YORKSHIRE GREATS

Great Achievers from Yorkshire's Past

COMPILED BY

Dawn G Robinson-Walsh

AURORA
PUBLISHING

Material extracted from:-
"Old Yorkshire" five volumes.
Published in 1882, originally edited by William Smith.

© AURORA PUBLISHING

ISBN: 1 85926 033 0

Distributed by: Aurora Enterprises Ltd.
Unit 9C, Bradley Fold Trading Estate,
Radcliffe Moor Road,
Bradley Fold,
BOLTON BL2 6RT
Tel: 0204 370753/2
Fax: 0204 370751

Compiled by: Dawn G Robinson-Walsh.

Printed
and bound by: Manchester Free Press,
Unit E3, Longford Trading Estate,
Thomas Street,
Stretford,
Manchester M32 0JT.

Front cover illustration: Charlotte Brontë.

*I*ntroduction

It is always interesting to read about other people's lives; that fascination is magnified when the people concerned are characters from the past, and people of great talent and craft. Yorkshire has been particularly fortunate in being the birthplace to men and women of talent, and this book is drawn from William Smith's five volumes on Yorkshire, written in 1882, which includes brief portraits of those whom he considered worthy at the time. Sadly, women are under-represented in his writings, and the only one included here is Charlotte Brontë, perhaps the most popular of the literary sisters, whose talent and renown is far-reaching and celebrated even today. The book includes achievers from all walks of life, some who changed history, and others who simply excelled at what they did. They include men such as John Wycliffe, the reformer, who translated the Bible into English and was a leading light of the Reformation, which dramatically changed the state of the Church in England. Also included are great industrialists and manufacturers, such as Sir Titus Salt, whose industrial village, Saltaire in Bradford, remains a monument to his merchant skills and his philanthropy. Back to the arts, the poet, Andrew Marvell, a metaphysical poet and satirist, is worthy of his place.

Yorkshire should be proud of her famous, industrious sons and daughters, and hopefully this slender edition will give a taste of Yorkshire talent and a desire to know more. If you enjoy this book, a companion volume, "Stories and Tales of Old Yorkshire" is also available.

Dawn G Robinson-Walsh

Contents

FRANK OATES-NATURALIST. 8

MATTHEW MURRAY-ENGINEER. 14

JAMES MONTGOMERY-POET. 23

HERBERT KNOWLES-POET. 29

MARSHAL-GENERAL WADE-ARMY COMMANDER. 31

GENERAL SIR RICHARD DEAN-ARMY COMMANDER 32

WILLIAM ETTY- ARTIST. 37

WILLIAM P.FRITH-ARTIST. 40

THOMAS CRESWICK-ARTIST. 42

JOHN HARLAND-AUTHOR. 43

CHARLOTTE BRONTE-AUTHOR. 47

JOHN JAMES-HISTORIAN. 55

DR JOHN FOTHERGILL-PHYSICIAN. 57

REV. JAMES HILDYARD-ACADEMIC CLERGYMAN. 66

JOHN SYKES-ANTIQUARY. 73

RALPH THORESBY-TOPOGRAPHER. 73

SIR MARTIN FROBISHER-BUCCANEER. 81

JOHN HOLLAND- JOURNALIST. 87

BISHOP JOHN ALCOCK-LORD CHANCELLOR. 96

PROFESSOR B F COCKER-ACADEMIC & MINISTER. 102

BISHOP PURSGLOVE-CLERGYMAN. 105

BISHOP BRIAN WALTON-BIBLICAL SCHOLAR. 109

JOHN WYCLIFFE- REFORMER. 111

ANDREW MARVELL-POET. 118

WILLIAM STERNDALE BENNETT. SCHOLAR OF MUSIC. 125

WILLIAM JACKSON, COMPOSER. 127

JOHN JACKSON, PORTRAIT PAINTER. 132

THOMAS PROCTOR, SCULPTOR. 132

WILLIAM LODGE, ENGRAVER. 133

TITUS SALT,INDUSTRIALIST. 135

JOHN GOWER, POET LAUREATE. 139

ROBERT COLLYER, POET & PREACHER. 140

JOHN NICHOLSON, POET. 145

JOHN REED APPLETON,POET & ANTIQUARY. 149

ROBERT BASTON, POET LAUREATE. 151

CHARLES WILLIAM SIKES, BANKER. 153

RICHARD THORNTON, AFRICAN EXPLORER. 158

JOHN TRAVIS,SURGEON & NATURALIST. 162

NICHOLAS SAUNDERSON,MATHEMATICIAN. 163

JOHN DAWSON, MATHEMATICIAN. 164

ABRAHAM SHARP, MECHANIC & MATHEMATICIAN. 165

ARCHBISHOP SHARP,CLERGYMAN. 167

JOSEPH GILLOTT,MANUFACTURER. 168

CHARLES FORREST,TOPOGRAPHER. 172

HENRY STOOKS SMITH,POLITICIAN & BOOK COLLECTOR.....174

STORIES & TALES OF
OLD YORKSHIRE

Originally edited by William Smith in 1883

Selected & Edited by Dawn Robinson-Walsh

FRANK OATES

A YORKSHIRE NATURALIST.

HE subject of our sketch, Mr. Frank Oates, was born in 1840. He was the son of Mr. Edward Oates, of Mean-woodside, near Leeds, a member of a family honoured for high principle and intelligence in successive genera-tions. At 20 years of age Frank entered at Christ Church, Oxford, his tastes leading him mainly though ·not exclusively to the Natural Science Schools, while his love of exercise, fresh air, and the country were from time to time almost passionately indulged, not, however, to the neglect of work, which was, on the contrary, pursued with only too great zeal, for his University career closed in a complete break-down of health and strength, which it took him some years to recover from. The moral drawn by himself in a letter to one of his brothers was—"Let me advise you not to do too many things." Good advice, which perhaps it would have been well for himself to act upon when trying to appropriate and assimilate the various matters of interest that claimed his attention in the wilds of South Africa. A trip to Central America, where he spent some months, and whence he passed to California and the Rocky Mountains, braced him up again, but only increased his longing for travel and all of life in its varied aspects which might thus be revealed and studied. It was during very early days at Oxford that he wrote—"I like everything that seems difficult of attainment," and his friends were not surprised to learn that he was off in March, 1873, for the Zambesi. Instead of following the usual route, he resolved on reaching the great goal of his ambition, the Victoria Falls, and unexplored country yet further north, by way of Natal. Thither his brother William accompanied him, intending himself to be away from England only about a year. On the 23rd of June, the party arrived at Pretoria, and Frank Oates, writing from thence, says:—After staying a few days at Ladysmith and Newcastle, we then got into the Transvaal Republic. Here in Pretoria are a great many English. The town itself, the seat of the government, does not contain a single good building. It is like some little frontier town in America. There is not even a book shop in it. The day we reached Pretoria, the mail, a fortnightly one, arrived from Pietermaritzburg with a paper containing English news, very bare items though, up to May 15th. Pretoria is a miserable little place, though the capital of the Transvaal." The travellers left Pretoria on the 30th of June for Bamangwato, and after three days' trekking to the north-west, crossed the Crocodile river, keeping at no great distance from its banks. Frank Oates, writing of this river, says :—" It is by far the most beautiful thing I have yet seen in South Africa," and in a letter he adds :—" The Crocodile (or Limpopo) river is a really beautiful river, its banks covered with fine trees.

Pretoria, Transvaal.

Continuing near its course for several days, still in a north-westerly direction, the brothers, on July 29th, reached Bamangwato, a Basuto settlement. There they fell in for the first time with missionaries (of the London Missionary Society). During the remainder of his sojourn in the African interior Frank Oates was repeatedly indebted to these gentlemen for counsel and help of various kinds. He gratefully acknowledges his obligations on these occasions, especially to the Rev. Messrs. Thomson and Mackenzie, of whom he saw the most, and the former of whom has, like himself, since died under the effects of overwork or work in an unhealthy climate. At Tati, in Matabele Land, the travellers separated, the younger Oates returning home by the route previously traversed, and Frank pushing on to the Matabele "capital." From this point he was thrown on his own resources, and one cannot but be struck with the courage,

9

patience, self-denial, and good humour which shone forth, as claims for each or all were made by the treachery, petty artifices, impudent demands, and occasional menaces of the monarch and the "meanest of his subjects." What was most trying of all was that after nearly endless troubles in actual progression, he was thrice turned back by officials when far on his way to the object of his aspirations and subject of his dreams, the Victoria Falls. Months were thus at different times lost, and, as he thought, wasted. After the third rebuff, his spirit was disposed for a while to acquiesce, and he seriously contemplated returning home, though still disbelieving in the danger

Limpopo or Crocodile River.

to life said to lurk in the country near the Zambesi, except indeed in certain months. He had been indignant at a trader who knew the country, and who in February, 1874, had said it would be a good thing for people travelling to have "portable coffins;" but he added, "I am thankful to say my health is excellent." Unhappily, as it seems to his friends, in November of the above year, when his plans were formed for proceeding southward, the arrival at Tati of some traders whom he knew revolutionised them all. They were bound for the Zambesi, but intended only to camp at a safe distance from it throughout the coming wet season. This latter fact he learned too late to induce him to withdraw from an engagement to join them, and accordingly the end of the year saw him within a few miles of the Falls. He fancied that the unhealthy season had not begun; the attraction was too strong, and his journal, under date of "New Year's Day, 1875," contained the triumphant yet characteristically simple entry—"After breakfast I visited the Falls—a day never to be forgotten." He remained some days in the immediate neighbourhood of the stupendous scenes, of which his note-book contained several sketches but no comments, and in a fortnight had rejoined the party who had stayed behind. It was now resolved to proceed southward, but within about ten days Frank Oates became ill (as two of his servants had done previously). For a few days it seemed as if he might throw off the fever, but on the 5th of

Mission Station, Shoshong, Bamangwato.

February, just before sunset, "the brave spirit sank peacefully to rest." Those who had watched his last hours chose, after kindly and thought-ful consultation, a spot for his grave, and there reverently placed him. "His was a burial which well became in its simplicity a true lover, like himself, of Nature and her wilds." The rest of the party then returned to Bamangwato, where the traveller's collections were placed in the hands of Mr. Mackenzie, the missionary, till the wishes of his friends in England could be obtained regarding them. A touching incident occurred upon the journey. "It appears that many miles after they had left the grave, one of Frank Oates's pointers—his favourite "Rail"—was found to be missing, and boys were sent back in search of him. These men sought long and wandered far in vain, till at length in their pursuit they got back even to the grave, and there, patiently watching, they found the devoted creature laid. A little longer, and he must inevitably have fallen a prey to lions or other wild beasts, but now he was taken down with his companion to Bamangwato, whence they were subsequently conveyed to England. And thus it happened that, whilst Frank Oates's friends at home were rejoicing at the speedy prospect of his return, and wholly unsuspicious of the truth, this faithful dog was watching, the sole mourner, by his grave."

"His love of nature generally, and of natural history in all its branches, was one of Frank Oates's earliest instincts; and to the study

Victoria Falls, Zambesi (The Outlet.)

of our English wild birds—their ways and haunts, their comings and their goings—he was especially devoted from boyhood. The pages of Waterton and Buffon, treating of wider fields of study, supplied his imagination at that period with richer food; and the plates of Audubon's Birds, when access could be had to them, were turned by him with feelings little short of reverence. From his earliest days he had resolved to visit those distant and, to him, still mysterious lands, where the page of nature was yet to the white man in great part an unread book; and those who, after his death in the full prime of manhood, witnessed the arrival at his English home of his large collections of natural history specimens, brought from the interior of South Africa by the devoted service of a friend, realised strangely how the boy's ambition had been fulfilled in after life, and felt that though cut off in the very perfection of his powers, the purpose of his being had not wholly failed. Those even who knew him best were surprised, indeed, when these evidences of his work abroad arrived, to see how much he had accomplished in the brief period—a little short of two years—of his absence. As, one after another, the packing-cases were opened, each in its turn afforded to the looker-on some fresh illustration of the untiring determination of the deceased traveller to make the very utmost of his opportunities whilst abroad. The voice that could alone have told the story of those collections, the hand that had brought them thus together, were silent and still in a far-distant grave ; but an

Camp in the Veldt.

utterance—the more pathetic because it was inaudible—seemed to go forth, unbidden, from those speechless records of devoted work and enterprise, and tell the secret tale of a life in earnest sympathy with nature curtailed—the hand, as it were, yet warm from its labours."

It seems that within about twenty months Frank Oates had amassed important collections of specimens in many departments of natural history, including large numbers of birds, reptiles, insects, and plants ; whilst some Bushman remains which he obtained towards the close of his wanderings cast valuable light, in the opinion of the late Professor Rolleston, on certain ethnological points of interest.

For a fuller account of the career of Mr. Oates, we would refer our readers to the volume entitled, "Matabele Land and the Victoria Falls," in which the brother of Mr. Oates has placed on record the life and experiences of the naturalist traveller in his wanderings in distant lands. To this gentleman (Mr. C. G. Oates), we are indebted for the illustrations which accompany this notice.

Faithful unto Death.

MATTHEW MURRAY

ABOUT a century ago, a young mechanic, who had just completed the term of his apprenticeship in Stockton, finding trade in that town coming to a standstill, with no prospect of immediate improvement, resolved to try his fortune in Leeds. Two reasons weighed with him in coming to this decision. He had married before he began to earn journeyman's wages, and the claims which others had upon him made it necessary that he should not remain in idleness. Then tidings had come north that attempts were being made to add to the industries of

14

Leeds ; and the Stockton mechanic, thrown out of work, was hopeful that in the Yorkshire town he would find an opening for his skill, in which he had some confidence, and possibly also scope for the development of an inventive talent of a kind that enabled him not only to discover defects in machinery but to suggest practical remedies. His trade was his only capital. It does not appear that he had money enough to pay the stage-coach fare, or to make the trip by water in one of the vessels that in those days made direct communication between the Tees and the Aire possible. So he took to the Great North Road, with a bundle on his back, and turning his face southward, trudged on afoot. How long he took to cover the distance between the two towns does not appear ; but it is known that he arrived in Leeds exhausted in purse and in body. Such a man coming a stranger into the borough to-day would doubtless be put down as a tramp, and be referred to the relieving-officer and to the vagrant shed. A century ago, however, it was no uncommon thing for workmen to drift about the country in this way ; and this poor traveller from Stockton, having come on an honest errand, staggered at the end of his long walk into the public room of the Bay Horse Inn, and paid his respects to the landlord. His case was this : He wanted rest and food and a place to sleep for a night or two, and if the landlord was willing to accept the word of a man who was penniless he would be repaid in full and with gratitude without doubt. Near to Adel, Mr. John Marshall had begun the manufacture of flax, and the new-comer was hopeful that there he would find a situation. All through his life afterwards, it must have been a pleasing reflection to the Bay Horse landlord that he did not question the man's word ; for the person to whom on this appeal he opened his heart and his house gave to the manufacture of flax in Leeds and elsewhere throughout England a stimulus which it has never lost, constructed machinery that rivalled and in some cases outranked that of Boulton and Watt, and made improvements in the steam engine in its application to locomotion which should not be forgotten at a time when the work of " the father of railways" has been brought into prominence. He built what is admitted by Stephenson's best biographer as the first locomotive engine ever successfully employed for commercial purposes. For one of his flax machines he received, at the hands of the Duke of Sussex, the gold medal of the Society of Arts ; and honours were bestowed upon him by the Governments of Russia and Sweden.

Notwithstanding facts like these, it is just possible that the majority of the readers to-day will not be able to recall the subject of this sketch. Great engineer as he was, there are historical works on the steam engine which bear no testimony of him whatever ; but his claims are fairly acknowledged in early works on the subject, and Mr. Smiles in his "Industrial Biography," and Mr. Galloway in "The Steam Engine and its Inventors," will not be consulted in vain for recognition of the great work Matthew Murray did. He was born in 1765, and his connection with Leeds, beginning with his interview with the landlord of the Bay Horse Inn, was continued until his death in 1826. Something in the appearance of the young man—his frank face, and his intelligent, honest statement, doubtless, of what he could do—impressed Mr. Marshall in his favour. He was engaged at once. Flax manufacture was not at the time in a prosperous state. The outlay was altogether out of proportion to the returns, and there was a prospect that the business in this neighbourhood would eventually be abandoned as a ruinous experiment. Young Murray, turning his attention to the machinery, was able from the outset to suggest improvements that were carried out with such benefit to his employer, that Mr. Marshall, first having given him a present of £20, soon saw the policy of making him first mechanic in the workshop. Murray having by this time made up his mind to settle in Leeds, sent to Stockton for his wife, rented a cottage at Black Moor, and for twelve years gave his whole services to Mr. Marshall. He continued as he began, adding inventions of his own to the machinery under his care, improving upon the inventions of others, and substituting inexpensive and simple processes in the spinning department for crude and costly modes of work. Fortunately, Mr. Marshall, who had himself a good knowledge of machinery, encouraged Murray in all his plans, so that the hope of the inventor that in Leeds he might find scope for the development of his mechanical talents was so far realised. In time, the Adel Mill became too small for its purpose, and the great manufactory at Holbeck, opened under the firm-name of Marshall and Benyon, was built. In time also, Murray saw that he might do still better work if in business himself; and in 1795 he became a partner with Mr. James Fenton and Mr. David Wood, and established an engineering and machine-making factory at Holbeck, Wood and Murray being the working partners. The arrangement was that Mr. Wood should take charge of the machinery, and Mr. Murray of the engine-making. At this period the chief engineering establishment in the country was the famous Soho Works at Birmingham, belonging to Boulton and Watt, whose productions were so far in advance of all others that they were not affected by competition. Mr. Murray's inventive genius, however, coupled with the fact that the machinery turned out from his establishment was remarkable for fine finish and an exquisite adjustment of parts, soon began to tell in favour of his firm. Orders came to Fenton, Wood, and Murray from all parts; and the demand rapidly increased when it became known that Mr. Murray had invented a contrivance by which he made use of the steam in the boiler to increase or decrease the draught of the fire. This invention was patented so early as 1799, and, with modifications, is still in use. It was followed by important improvements in the slide valve and in the air pump, the adoption of a method of fixing the wheels so as to produce motion alternately in perpendicular and horizontal directions, and other ingenious arrangements. In carrying out these changes Mr. Murray invented a planing machine, such a piece of mechanism having been found necessary to produce the requisite evenness of surface in the valve work. The result was that Boulton and Watt became sensible that a formidable rival to their enterprise had arisen in Leeds; and Mr. Murdock, their managing superintendent and a competent engineer, came down and inspected Fenton, Wood, and Murray's establishment. Mr. Murray received his visitor very cordially, concealed nothing from him, and gave him free access to the works. The visit was, indeed, one in which Mr. Murray took a special delight, he being of an exceedingly frank disposition, and never happier than when he found himself in the company of any one of similar tastes to himself. What passed between Mr. Murdock and his employers on his return to Birmingham cannot be told; but it may be guessed at from the fact that in a short time thereafter a large tract of land ajoining Fenton, Wood, and Murray's workshops was purchased for Boulton and Watt. This was done, it has been asserted, to prevent any extension of premises on the part of the now rival firm ; although it may have been for the purpose of erecting a branch of the Birmingham establishment in Leeds. In either event the object would be the same, and if the latter idea was ever entertained it was never carried out, for the acquired ground remained unused for nearly half a century, and only within the last few years has it changed hands. Murray returned Murdock's visit on one occasion while on his way back to Leeds from London. Murdock gladly received his Leeds friend, and invited him and Mrs. Murray to dinner, but expressed his regret that he could not show Mr. Murray over the Soho Works, as there was a rule against admitting any one in the trade. Under the circumstances, such treatment was felt by Murray to be little better than an insult; the invitation to dinner was courteously declined ; Leeds was reached without further delay; and, despite the effort made to prevent the extension of the works, Murray, stimulated, no doubt, by the slight he had received, applied himself with such good purpose to his business, that his firm went on increasing in reputation and in power.

Mr. Murray took up his residence in Holbeck, at a place within convenient access from his works. He improved his dwelling as he improved everything else in which he took an interest. One of the changes he made was the introduction of a heating apparatus, which secured for the house the name of "Steam Hall," by which it was long known. Thither one evening, during the unsettled period when "General Ludd" and his following waged their foolish and futile campaign against the progress of machinery, came a crowd of angry men, threatening destruction to the building and injury to the inmates unless Mr. Murray should cease to turn out inventions that, in their short-sightedness, they imagined were calculated to bring idleness, and not fresh fields of labour to the toiler. Mr. Murray was not at home. His wife was, and she was a brave woman. She looked out from a window, and betrayed no sign of fear. Having first heard the angry words that were addressed to her, she calmly replied that she was able

MATTHEW MURRAY,

Engineer.

to defend herself, and levelling a pistol, fired it at the crowd. None of the besiegers were hurt, but they were all well frightened, and took to immediate flight. Never again was Steam Hall visited on a like errand.

Mr. Murray naturally took a deep interest in Trevithick's attempts to construct a locomotive engine, and, like the other engineers of his day, he endeavoured to account for the defects which detracted from the practical value of Trevithick's invention. He failed to discover the features which led to such a brilliant success in Stephenson's " Rocket," but he made a greater advance on Trevithick's plans than any other engineer of that day, and he undoubtedly, as Dr. Smiles admits, made the first locomotive that regularly worked upon any railway. It is noteworthy, also, that Stephenson followed Murray's mode of construction up to a certain point. Indeed, between the working parts of Stephenson's first engine (Locomotion) and that built by Matthew Murray the resemblance is close; the essential points of difference are in the driving wheels and in the roadway rather than in the engine itself. Trevithick constructed several engines, each showing an improvement on its predecessor; but the inventor was singularly unfortunate in the trials to which he subjected the engines, and eventually, after an expenditure of a great deal of money, threw up the problem he came so near solving. The last of these trials was made in London in 1808, on a small, enclosed circular line, constructed for the purpose on a portion of the site now occupied, singularly enough, for railway purposes—namely, the Euston Station. On this occasion the engine is said to have made speed at the rate of about twelve miles an hour, and Trevithick declared that on a straight line a speed of twenty miles an hour could have been maintained. The experiment demonstrated what was perhaps a still more important fact—that an absolutely straight line for a railroad was not essential. The breaking of a rail and the running away of the engine at a tangent, when it overturned, stopped a trial that had lasted some weeks. And from this time Trevithick did not interest himself directly in locomotive schemes. The next locomotive put to a practical test in England was the one built by Matthew Murray.* It was constructed for the conveyance of coal from the Middleton Colliery to Leeds, and is best known as Blenkinsop's engine. Mr. Blenkinsop was the manager of the colliery, and in his name the patent was taken out (April 10th,

---

* Next in importance to Watt's improvements on the engine, may be reckoned Mr. Matthew Murray's, of Leeds, on the self-acting apparatus attached to the boiler which regulated the intensity of the fire under the boiler, an invention of great practical use, and among the few which are still used on all well-constructed boilers. He also introduced several improvements in the details of the many beautiful engines which were constructed in his great manufactory at Leeds.—*From Stuart's History of the Steam Engine* (1824.)

Much was done by Mr. Murray, of the firm of Fenton, Wood, and Murray, of Leeds, in improving several parts of the steam engine, which he included in his patents of 1791, 1801, and 1802.—*Grier's Mechanics' Dictionary.*

1811). To him doubtless belongs the credit of having suggested to Murray the idea of constructing an engine for the purpose mentioned, and of securing the necessary consent and capital from his employers at the colliery. The engine itself was Murray's, and showed this manifest improvement as compared with Trevithick's, that it was provided with two double-acting cylinders. A regular and steady action was thus obtained without a fly-wheel. The idea was to run the engine on a rack-rail, into which a pinion-wheel would fit, and in accordance with this notion the engine and railway were constructed. The engine was provided in addition with a double set of smooth wheels, so that the purpose served by the pinion and the rack-rail was in the

Blenkinsop's Engine.
From an old engraving in the possession of T. W. Embleton, Esq., C.E., Methley.

nature of leverage or purchase. By this means the difficulty of working upon gradients was effectively overcome. The patent is somewhat quaintly worded. It sets forth that "John Blenkinsop, of Middleton, in the parish of Rothwell, in the county of York, coal-viewer," had secured it for having invented "certain mechanical means by which the conveyance of coals, minerals, and other articles is facilitated, and the expense is rendered less than heretofore." The engine itself is not described in the patent, although it was probably built at the time the instrument was secured. At any rate, it was seen in experimental operation in the engineering yard a year or two before the public trial took place. The following paragraph, descriptive of the opening of the railway, appears in the *Leeds Mercury* of June 27th, 1812 :—

On Wednesday last [June 24th] a highly interesting experiment was made with a machine constructed by Messrs. Fenton, Murray, and Wood, of this place, under the direction of Mr. John Blenkinsop, the patentee, for the purpose of substituting the agency of steam for the use of horses in the conveyance of coals, on the Iron-rail-way from the mines of J. C. Brandling, Esq., of Middleton, to Leeds. This machine is in fact a steam engine of four horses' power, which, with the assistance of cranks turning a cog-wheel, and iron cogs placed at one side of the rail-way, is capable of moving, when lightly loaded, at the speed of ten miles an hour. At four o'clock in the afternoon the machine ran from the Coal-staith to the top of Hunslet Moor, where six, and afterwards eight, waggons of coals, each weighing 3¼ tons, were hooked to the back part. With this immense weight, to which as it approached the town was super-added about 50 of the spectators mounted upon the waggons, it set off on its return to the Coal-staith, and performed the journey, a distance of about a mile and a half, principally on a dead level, in 23 minutes, without the slightest accident. The experiment, which was witnessed by thousands of spectators, was crowned with complete success ; and when it is considered that this invention is applicable to all rail-roads, and that upon the works of Mr. Brandling alone the use of 50 horses will be dispensed with, and the corn necessary for the consumption of at least 200 men saved, we cannot forbear to hail the invention as of vast public utility, and to rank the inventor amongst the benefactors of his country.

Another paragraph in the same paper two months later describes " Mr. Blenkinsop's machine" as being in full activity. The engine does not seem to have broken down seriously at any time. Other engines of the same kind were built by Mr. Murray, and in 1813 one of them was forwarded to Newcastle and was used on a railway leading from the Kenton and Coxlodge Colliery to a point on the Tyne below Walker. It was doubtless seen in operation here by George Stephenson, and either before or after that time Stephenson had made the acquaintance of Murray, and become familiar with the strange mechanism that subsequently in his hands revolutionised the carrying trade of the country. Until a better locomotive was found at work, the "machine" at the Middleton Colliery was a sight which attracted many visitors. Among other notabilities who came to see it was the Grand Duke Nicholas (afterwards Emperor) of Russia. This was in 1816. On that occasion the power of the engine was shown in the conveyance of thirty loaded coal waggons at a speed of about three miles and a quarter an hour.

The construction of these engines did not interrupt Mr. Murray's work in the production of other kinds of machinery. He continued to put his experience at Mr. Marshall's mill to practical account by adding to his improvements on the apparatus for the manufacture of flax. The gold medal of the Society of Arts was given to him for a heckling machine, patented after he had been some years at work for himself, and this and his other inventions in connection with the same branch of industry gave to the British linen trade a supremacy which it has continued to hold. He designed all the machine tools used in his establishments, and made similar articles for other firms, and so started a branch of engineering for which Leeds has become famous. Leeds is also largely indebted to him for the introduction of gas into the town, the supply being poor and unreliable until he remodelled the retorts and condensers. Other towns profited by improvements like these, and it is not too much to claim for Matthew Murray a prominent part in the promotion of the industrial triumphs of England. There ought to be in Leeds, at least, some lasting memorial of him, "not to perpetuate a name"—(to quote and slightly alter a part of the epitaph on his great contemporary)—"which should endure while the peaceful arts flourish, but to show that mankind have learned to honour those who best deserve their gratitude."

Mr. Murray lies buried in the cemetery attached to St. Matthew's Church, Holbeck. Over his grave rises to a height of fifteen feet or so from the pedestal a cast-iron obelisk—an unpretentious memorial, but the most conspicuous object in the churchyard. On a panel is this inscription :—

IN A VAULT UNDERNEATH
ARE DEPOSITED THE REMAINS OF
MATTHEW MURRAY
CIVIL ENGINEER OF HOLBECK,
WHO DIED THE XX. OF FEBRUARY
MDCCCXXVI., AGED LX. YEARS.
ALSO OF MARY, HIS WIFE
WHO DIED THE XVIII. OF DECEMBER
MDCCCXXXVI., AGED LXXI. YEARS.

An epitaph this, as modest as the man, claiming no more for him than he claimed for himself; but there is an impressive significance in the fact that the engineering trade of Leeds of which Matthew Murray was the founder has some of its largest workshops within sight and hearing at the obelisk; that not far off is the huge establishment where the earliest successes of this great inventor were won, and that from the cemetery may be seen in unceasing activity and in its latest development that locomotive machinery which he was the first man to bring into practical and remunerative use. In such signs we have his fittest epitaph; but his memory in these things has not been cherished as it should have been, nor does his resting-place at Holbeck appear to be a shrine many visitors find their way to. The writer had to beat a path through a wilderness of weeds to get at it. In the same tomb, according to another inscription, are interred the remains of Margaret, wife of Richard Jackson, of Leeds, a daughter of Murray, who died in 1840. Another daughter was married to Mr. J. O. March, of Leeds, and in Mr. March's possession is the only portrait of his father-in-law that is known to have been taken. A third daughter was married to Mr. Charles G. Maclea, who was elected Mayor of Leeds in 1844, but retired, after serving a short time, in consequence of ill-health. A grandson of Murray (Matthew Murray Jackson) is an eminent engineer in Austria, who has recently obtained titular distinction for his services from the Emperor of that country.

Leeds.   W. S. CAMERON.

JAMES MONTGOMERY

SHEFFIELD has been poetically fortunate. It has had the honour, not to give birth to two eminent poets—a mere accident, but to produce them. Neither Montgomery nor Elliott was born in Sheffield; but there their minds, tastes, and reputations grew. In both poets are strongly recognisable the intellectual features of a manufacturing town. They are both of a popular and liberal tendency of mind. They, or rather their spirits and characters, grew amid the physical sufferings and the political struggles of a busy and high-spirited population, and by these circumstances all the elements of freedom and patriotism were strengthened to full growth in their bosoms. Montgomery came upon the public stage, both as a poet and a political writer, long before Elliott, though the difference of their ages was not so great as might be supposed from this fact, being only about ten years.

James Montgomery was born November 4th, 1771, in the little town of Irvine, in Ayrshire. The house at the time of his birth, and till his fifth year, was a very humble one. His father was the Moravian minister there, and probably had not a large congregation. When sixty years of age, the poet visited his birthplace, and was received there by the provost and magistrates of the town with great honour; in his own words, " the heart of all Irvine seemed to be moved on the occasion, and every soul of it, old and young, rich and poor, to hail me to my birthplace." Accompanied by his townsmen, he visited the cottage of his birth, and was surprised to find the interior marked by a memorial of his having been born there. In his fifth year he returned with his parents to Grace Hill, a settlement of the Moravian Brethren, near Ballymena, in the county of Antrim, in Ireland; and where his parents had resided previously to the year of the poet's birth. When between six and seven he was removed to the seminary of the Brethren at Fulneck, in Yorkshire. In the year 1783, his parents were sent out as missionaries to the West Indies, to preach to the poor slave the consoling doctrine of another and a better world, "where the wretched hear not the voice of the oppressor," and "where the servant is free from his master." There they both died. One lies in the Island of Barbadoes, the other in Tobago.

In the Fulneck academy, amongst a people remarkable for their ardour in religion, and their industry in the pursuit of useful learning, James Montgomery received his education. He was intended for the ministry, and his preceptors were every way competent to the task of preparing him for the important office for which he was designed. His

James Montgomery.

studies were various: the French, German, Latin, and Greek languages; history, geography, and music; but a desire to distinguish himself as a poet soon interfered with the plan laid out for him. When ten years old he began to write verses, and continued to do so with unabated ardour till the period when he quitted Fulneck, in 1787; they were chiefly on religious subjects. Fulneck, the chief settlement of the Moravian Brethren in England, at which we have seen that Montgomery continued till his sixteenth year, is about eight miles from Leeds. It was built about 1760, which was near the time of the death of Count Zinzendorf. It was then in a fine and little inhabited country. It is now in a country as populous as a town, full of tall chimneys vomiting out enormous masses of soot rather than smoke, and covering the landscape as with an eternal veil of black mist. The villages are like towns for extent. Stone and smoke are equally abundant. The situation of the settlement, were it not for these circumstances, is fine. It has something monastic about it. The establishment consists of one range of buildings, though built at various times. There are the school, chapel, master's house, &c., in the centre, of stone, and a sisters' and brothers' house, of brick, at each end, with various cottages behind. A fine broad terrace-walk extends along the front, a furlong in length, being the length of the buildings; from which you may form a conception of the stately scale of the place, which is one-eighth of a mile long. From this descend the gardens, play-grounds, &c., down the hill for a great way, and private walks are thence continued as far again, to the bottom of the valley, where they are further continued along the brook side, amongst the deep

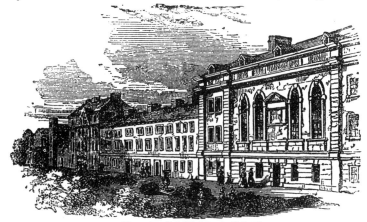

Moravian Establishment, Fulneck.

woodlands. The valley is called the Tong valley; the brook the Tong; and Mr. Tempest's house, on the opposite slope, Tong Hall.

When Montgomery removed from Fulneck, the views of his friends were so far changed, that we find him placed by them in a retail shop at Mirfield. Here, though he was treated with great kindness, and had only too little business and too much leisure to attend to his favourite pursuit, he became exceedingly disconsolate, and after remaining in his new situation about a year and a half he privately absconded, and with less than five shillings in his pocket, and the wide world before him, began his career in pursuit of fame and fortune. His ignorance of mankind, the result of his retired and religious education,—the consequent simplicity of his manners, and his forlorn appearance,—exposed him to the contempt of some, and to the compassion of others, to whom he applied. The brilliant bubble of patronage, wealth, and celebrity, which floated before his imagination, soon burst, and on the fifth day of his travels he found a situation similar to the one he had left, at the village of Wath, near Rotherham. From this place he removed to London, having prepared his way by sending a volume of his manuscript poems to Mr. Harrison, then a bookseller in Paternoster-row. Mr. Harrison, who was a man of correct taste and liberal disposition, received him into his house, and gave him the greatest encouragement to cultivate his talents, but none to publish his poems ; seeing, as he observed, no probability that the author would acquire either fame or fortune by appearing at that time before the public. The remark was just; but it conveyed the most unexpected and afflicting information to our youthful poet, who yet knew little of the world, except from books, and who had permitted his imagination to be dazzled with the accounts which he had read of the splendid success and magnificent patronage which poets had formerly experienced. He was so disheartened by this circumstance, that, on occasion of a misunderstanding with Mr. Harrison, he, at the end of eight months, quitted the metropolis and returned to Wath, where he was received with a hearty welcome by his former employer. From Wath, where Montgomery had sought only a temporary residence, he removed in 1792, and engaged himself with Mr. Gales of Sheffield, as an assistant in his business of auctioneer. Gales was also a bookseller, and printed a newspaper, in which popular politics were advocated with great zeal and ability. To this paper Montgomery contributed essays and verses occasionally ; but though politics sometimes engaged the service of his hand, the Muses had his whole heart, and he sedulously cultivated their favour ; though no longer with those false, yet animating hopes, which formerly stimulated his exertions. In 1794, when Mr. Gales left England, a gentleman, to whom Montgomery was an almost entire stranger, enabled him to undertake the publication of the paper on his own account.

For the long period of half a century he was essentially bound up with the literary and social progress of Sheffield, his adopted home. Editing, for the greater part of that period, the *Iris* newspaper, on which his name and writings conferred a popular celebrity ; and from time to time sending forth one of his volumes of poetry, there is no question that the influence of his taste and liberal opinions has been greatly instrumental in the growth of that spirit of intelligence and moral culture which highly distinguish Sheffield. With the religious world, as was to be expected, James Montgomery has always stood in high esteem and in the most friendly relation. Besides the works already mentioned, Montgomery published Songs of Zion in 1822 ; Prose by a Poet, 1824 ; A Poet's Portfolio, 1835. His collected works, in three vols., in 1836. Through his own exertions, the proceeds of his pen, and a pension of £150 a-year, in testimony of his poetic merit, the poor orphan who set out from the little shop at Mirfield to seek fame and fortune with less than five shillings in his pocket, for some years retired to an enjoyment of both ; and no man ever reached the calm sunshine of life's evening with a purer reputation, or a larger share of the grateful affection of his townsmen, or of the honour of his country-men in general.

Strangers visiting Sheffield will have a natural curiosity to see where Montgomery so many years resided, and whence he sent forth his poems and his politics. That spot is in the Hartshead; one of the most singular situations for such a man and purpose often to be met with. Luckily, it was in the centre of the town, and not far to seek. Going up the High-street, various passages under the houses lead to one common centre,--the Hartshead,--a sort of *cul de sac*, having no

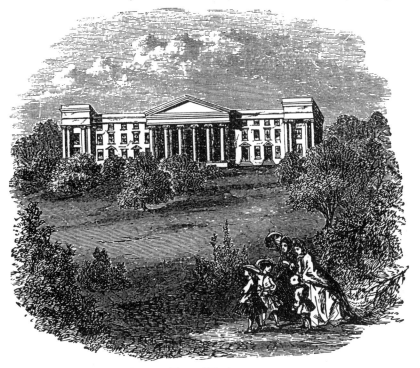

Home of Montgomery.

carriage road through, but only one into it, and that not from the main street. The shop, which used to be the *Iris* office, is of an odd ogee shape, at the end of a row of buildings. It has huge, ogee-shaped windows, with great dark-green shutters. The door is at the corner, making it a three-cornered shop. It was, at the time of my visit, a pawnbroker's shop, the door and all round hung with old garments. The shelves were piled with bundles of pawned clothes, ticketed. The houses round this strange hidden court, in which it stands, are nearly all public-houses, as the Dove and Rainbow, and the like, with low eating-houses, and dens of pettifogging lawyers; and, strange to say, even the pawnbroker's shop was afterwards converted into another beer-house! But, leaving the beer-house of the Harts-head, we shall find the poet of religion and refinement residing at the Mount, on the Glossop road, the *West End* of Sheffield. It is, I suppose, at least a mile and a half from the old *Iris* office, and is one

Tomb of Montgomery.

regular ascent all the way. The situation is lovely, lying high; and there are many pleasant villas built on the sides of the hill in their ample pleasure grounds, the abodes of the wealthy manufacturers. The Mount, *par excellence*, is the house, or rather terrace, where Mont-gomery lived. It is a large building, with a noble portico of six fine Ionic columns, so that it seems a residence fit for a prince. It stands in ample pleasure grounds, and looks over a splendid scene of hills and valleys. The rooms enjoy this fine prospect over the valleys of the

Sheaf and Porter, which, however, was obscured while I was there with the smoke blowing from the town.

Montgomery died at the Mount, April 30th, 1854, in the eighty-third year of his age. His townspeople honoured him by a public funeral, and he was interred in a beautiful spot of the cemetery, near the western end of the church ; one of his own beautiful hymns being sung over the uncovered grave, at the conclusion of the usual burial service, by the choir of the parish church and the children of the boys' and girls' charity-schools, to which the poet had long been a benefactor, and to which he left bequests in his will. With a wisdom founded not on calculation, but on a sacred sense of duty, Montgomery made even his ambition subservient to his aspirations as a Christian, and he thus reared for himself a pedestal in the poetic Walhalla of England peculiarly his own. The longer his fame endures, and the wider it spreads, the better it will be for virtue and for man.

London. WILLIAM HOWITT.

HERBERT KNOWLES

A YOUTHFUL genius, who owes to a single composition his position among the poets of Yorkshire, was born at Gomersal, near Bradford, in 1798. His parents dying in his infancy, he, along with two brothers, was left almost destitute. Herbert should have entered a merchant's counting-house in Liverpool ; but his abilities becoming manifest, a subscription of £20 a year was made towards his education on condition that his friends should contribute £30 more. He was accordingly placed at the celebrated Grammar School of Richmond, and whilst there he evinced powers of no ordinary kind, including that poetical talent which has rendered his name conspicuous. When he quitted school his friends were unable to advance any more money towards his education, so to help himself he wrote a poem and sent it to Southey, with a history of his case, and asked permission to dedicate it to the Laureate. Southey, finding the poem " brimful of promise," made inquiries of Herbert's instructor, and received the highest character of the youth. He then answered the application of Knowles, entreated him to avoid present publication, and promised to do something better than receive his dedication. He subscribed at once £10 per annum towards the failing £30, and procured similar subscriptions from the poet Rogers and Lord Spencer. On receiving the news of his good fortune, young Knowles wrote to his protector a letter, remarkable for much more than the gratitude which pervaded every line. He remembered that Kirke White had gone to the University countenanced and supported by patrons, and that to pay back the debt he owed them he wrought day and night, until his delicate frame gave way, and his life became the penalty of his devotion. Herbert Knowles felt that he

29

could not make the same desperate efforts, and he deemed it his first duty to say so. He promised to do what he could, assured his friends that he would not be idle, and that, if he could not reflect upon them any extraordinary credit, he would certainly do them no disgrace. Within two months after writing this letter the hopes which he had excited, and in some measure gratified. were extinguished by his severe illness and sudden death at Gomersal, February 17th, 1817, when he was only nineteen years of age. He left behind him a manuscript volume of poems, the earliest of which were published in the "Literary Gazette" for 1824 ; but neither that nor any others are at all comparable to his poem, "The Three Tabernacles"—a piece which Montgomery says "ought to endear the memory of the author. Truly, he built a monument more durable than brass in compiling these casual lines, with little prospect of pleasing anybody but himself and a circle of juvenile friends." The reader will please to remember that these are the verses of a schoolboy, and he will then judge what might have been expected from one who was capable of writing with such strength and originality upon the tritest of all subjects. The lines referred to may be read in Chambers's " Cyclopædia of Literature," Vol II., p. 411.

Pudsey.   S. RAYNER.

MARSHAL-GENERAL WADE

ARSHAL-GENERAL WADE was commander of one division of the army sent to oppose the entrance into England of Prince Charles in '45. His place of rendezvous was Newcastle, and his men were gathered from the northern counties, whilst the Duke of Cumberland collected his from the midlands, and the occasion of his encampment in Meanwood Road would doubtless be when he was marching his troops northward. He held a command also in the expedition against the Old Pretender in '15, and was in service fifty-eight years, dying in 1751, at the age of eighty. After the suppression of the rebellion of '15, he was left, for several years, Commander-in-Chief in Scotland, in which capacity he employed his men in constructing a series of military roads through the Highlands, in hitherto inacessible places, where there had previously been nothing but trackways, almost impassable in winter. These roads so delighted the natives that, in grateful commemoration they set up a stone, inscribed—

> Had you seen but these roads before they were made,
> You would lift up your hands and bless General Wade;

which would seem as if it had been composed by one of the Sister Isle. Marshal Wade came of an illustrious race. His earliest known ancestor was Wada, a Saxon noble of the eighth century, who inhabited a castle near Whitby. He was of gigantic stature; was one of the conspirators who murdered Æthelred, King of Northumbria; was defeated in battle at Whalley, in Lancashire, by Ardulph, Æthelred's successor; died soon after, and was buried in a hill between two stones seven feet high and twelve feet apart. A legend informs us that he had a cow for his wife, who for some cause or other had to go daily to a distant moor to be milked. As the way thither was rough and uneven, Wada set to

31

work to make a level road for her convenience, she bringing the stones in her apron. It chanced one day that her apron-string gave way, and the stones she was conveying, some twenty cart-loads, fell to the earth, and there they remained until recently, a monument of her industry and strength. The road is still in existence, and is called to this day "Wade's Cawsey." One of his wife's ribs may be seen in Mulgrave Castle, but some unbelieving sceptics contend that it is the bone of a whale. It may be presumed that it is from this remote ancestor that General Wade inherited his talent for road-making. From this redoubtable hero descended the Wades of New Grange, near Leeds, with whom General Wade was connected, but how nearly or how remotely is not apparent. Of a collateral branch was Henry Wade, of King's Cross, near Leeds, whose brother Anthony married, in 1590, Judith, daughter of Thos. Foxcroft, of New Grange, and had issue, with five daughters, Benjamin, of New Grange, and John, of King's Cross. Benjamin, who d.s.p. 1671, built the mansion at New Grange in 1626. He was a zealous Loyalist, and contributed £10,000 to the exchequer of Charles I. during the Civil Wars. John, his brother, who died in 1645, married Mary, daughter of John Waterhouse, of Woodhouse, Leeds. Anthony, his second son, of King's Cross, served the office of Mayor of Leeds in 1676, and died 1683. Benjamin, his son, of New Grange, married Anne, daughter of Walter Calverley, of Calverley, whose elder sons d.v.p. and s.p. Walter, his fifth son, succeeded; rebuilt the mansion at New Grange 1752, and died 1757. Walter, his second son, married Anne, daughter and heiress of Robert Allanson, of the Royd, Halifax, and died 1771. Benjamin, his third son (the two elder having died young), succeeded, and died 1792, having had issue three daughters, all of whom died young.

London.   F. Ross, F.R.H.S.

GENERAL SIR RICHARD DEAN

ABOUT the year 1600 William Dean was a dyer in Swinegate, Leeds. In his hands trade had prospered sufficiently to enable him to become a freeholder. The premises wherein he carried on his business were his own; they were situate behind those mills in Swinegate then, as now, called the "King's Mills," because they belonged to the Crown. Wm. Lindley, Esquire, of Leathley, the farmer of the mills under Queen Elizabeth, chose to pick a quarrel with the prosperous dyer, who had increased his premises in the direction of the royal property. Dean had erected a new building over against the mill-wheel, and this act had given offence to Lindley, who forthwith commenced a law-suit against the dyer, on the ground that, although erected upon Dean's land, the new building was injurious to the interests of the Crown, inasmuch as it prevented the sun from shining upon the mill-wheels in winter. The suit was tried at York, but the unsympathising jurymen, who could not be brought to see the reason why her Majesty's mill-wheels required the mocking, heatless rays of a winter sun to fall upon them, gave a verdict in favour of the dyer. This protest against tyranny supported by regal power, may be taken as an assurance that the Deans were men of indomitable resolution of purpose, for there were few men who dared to oppose her most gracious Majesty Elizabeth, Queen of England, France, and Ireland.*

Richard Dean, the subject of this memoir, is said by Wilson to have been the son or grandson of the above William; we incline to consider him the latter. Than this bald statement of the reluctant chronicler we know nothing more of the future hero until we find him a great and prominent man, whose actions are noticed in the chronicles of the age in which he lived and moved. Of his parentage, of his boyhood, of the development of his mind, of the inclination of his thoughts, of his early exploits, and of his early avocations, we know no more than if he had never lived. Heath is the only historian who speaks as to his origin. In that writer's account of the Regicides, we learn that Dean "was formerly a hoyman's servant at Ipswich, and when the war began was a matross in the train of artillery, and rose to a captain's command therein; and was famous first at the siege of Exeter, and being a cross fellow, was thought fit to be one of Cromwell's complices, to execute his plots against his Sovereign's life." The exact amount of truth contained in this statement we cannot point out. If ever Dean was a hoyman's servant at Ipswich, we are at a loss to explain how he became such; but that he was famous first at the siege of Exeter we can deny. The city of Exeter was delivered to Lord Fairfax on the 3rd of April, 1646, yet two years previous to that event Dean was an officer of some note in the army of the Earl of Essex, and his name appears among those of the officers of that army who signed the attestation concerning the surrender to the King at Lestithiel, in the month of August, 1644. In the "Squire Papers" published by Carlyle, the names of two persons, H. Deane and R. Deane, are given amongst those who were "hearty" to the cause; and one of these was captain of a troop—of Ironsides probably. As Dean's name does not appear among the names of officers of the first Parliamentary army, we must suppose he joined the service as a volunteer, zealous, but ignorant of military matters, after hostilities had actually commenced.

---

* This William Dean is the last of his race whom we can clearly show to have been settled in Leeds. Wilson, the antiquary, who succeeded Thoresby as the historian of the town, and continued to chronicle events until the middle of the eighteenth century, possessed the documents referring to Dean's law-suit, and had an opportunity of learning the leading facts relating to the family. But he did not do so, and the reason is perfectly obvious. Wilson was a Royalist of the narrowest and most bigoted kind, the Deans were Parliamentarians of the most uncompromising and sinful caste; therefore it was through political delinqencies, especially those of the one great member of their family, that no account of them should be recorded.

Two years of hard fighting had expired before Dean raised himself into historic notice. When Fairfax and Cromwell were chasing Rupert's broken army from Marston Moor, Dean was with the Earl of Essex rapidly winning victories for the Parliament in the distant counties of Devon and Cornwall.

It was during the campaign of 1645 that Dean established his military renown, and commenced that close friendship with Cromwell which terminated only in death. He fought with Cromwell at Naseby ; he shared in the triumphant march through the western counties ; he took a prominent part in the siege of Bristol, as comptroller of the ordnance ; he was one who dictated terms to Lord Hopton at Truro ; and he stood before Oxford to force Charles into submission when he had retreated there as to the last place in his kingdom which could offer him even a temporary asylum.

After the termination of the war, when it was urged there was no necessity for the maintenance of a body of soldiers larger than was required to prosecute the Irish war, and preserve order in the kingdom, Dean was appointed to the command of the artillery which was to be sent into Ireland. The peculiar turn military matters were taking in England, through the dispute between the army and the Parliament, seems to furnish the reason why he did not go. The army was Republican ; the opponents of the army were Royalists ; and as Dean was a Republican of the most uncompromising caste, it was only to be expected that he would remain at home where his counsel and advice might further the grand object of all his efforts. In all the important transactions, therefore, which preceded the execution of the King, we find Dean taking a prominent part on the side of the army and against those who sympathised with monarchy. He was colonel of a regiment of foot, under Cromwell, at the siege of Pembroke Castle ; he was again with him at the battle of Preston, Aug. 20th, 1648, when Oliver defeated the Scotch under the Duke of Hamilton.

On the 23rd of December the Commons voted that the King should be brought to trial. In the interval between the purging of the House of Commons and the passing of this vote, Dean had been one of the few with whom Cromwell was wont " to consider and confer how the settlement of the kingdom might be best effected." Dean's most unqualified advice would be in favour of the erection of a Republic. With this predisposition to put away the poor tyrant whom he had so strenuously helped to crush, Richard Dean was appointed one of the judges for the trying of the King, by the Act for erecting a High Court of Justice. He sedulously attended the several meetings of the Court, and signed his name to the King's death-warrant in bold, regular characters, very unlike those of a hoyman's servant.

When Cromwell called together a Parliament, Colonels Dean, Popham, and Blake were transferred from the land-service to the navy, and for some months they were in command of naval squadrons guarding the Channel, or watching the coasts of Ireland, where Rupert had taken that part of the English navy which still adhered to the King; where Ormond upheld the Royal cause with an army of considerable force; and where Cromwell was smiting his enemies with a strong and terrible hand. In March, 1650-1, Dean, Popham, and Blake were, by Act of Parliament, constituted Admirals and Generals of the Fleet, but when Charles Stuart attempted to make war upon the Commonwealth, Dean again took up his military command, and we find him acting a distinguished part at that "crowning success," the battle of Worcester.

When the naval war broke out between the English and the Dutch, Dean entered upon his command as an Admiral conjointly with General Monk. What his knowledge of naval affairs was at the outset of his naval career we cannot say; but if he was not an expert seamen, he appears to have been very apt to learn the duties of one.

The first great engagement with the Dutch was Dean's last. It commenced on the 2nd day of June, 1653, and at the first broadside, Dean was slain by a cannon ball which struck him in the breast. He was standing by the side of Monk when he fell, and his death seems to have been the cause of some consternation to the seamen of his ship. Monk covered the dead body with his cloak, and commanded the seamen to attend to their duty. A two days' action brought a complete victory to the English. Van Tromp, the most experienced naval officer of the day, saw his fleet taken or dispersed, and himself compelled to fly. The rejoicings of the English were greatly saddened by the death of Dean. In the report of the action which Monk transmitted to the Commissioner of the Admiralty he speaks of Dean as "an honest and able servant to this Commonwealth." The Admiral's mutilated body was taken to Greenwich, where it was received with mournful sadness. The 23rd of June (N.S. 3rd of July) was set apart by the English Parliament as a day of devotion and thanksgiving for their great victory, and it was generally kept throughout the city. On the 24th the Admiral was buried. The corpse was placed on board a barge, which was followed up the river by a procession of barges and boats, all in mourning equipage. As the procession passed along, the ships in the river discharged their guns, the batteries of the Tower thundered forth their dismal salute, and the solemn peal was continued by other guns placed on the banks of the river even up to the Abbey. The arrangements of Dean's funeral seem to have been those afterwards observed at the burial of his famous comrade, Blake. After the procession had landed at Westminster Bridge it passed through a guard of several regiments of soldiers, drawn up to do the last military honours to the deceased commander. Cromwell himself was there with the chief men of his Government. All the pomp and ceremony of military parade were exhausted to do honour to his memory. The corpse was carried through New Palace Yard to the Abbey, and was interred among the bodies of the greatest men of the land in the chapel of Henry VII. It remained there in quiet repose until the 12th Sept.,

1661, when the returned King dragged forth the mouldering bones, along with those of many other Republican heroes, and threw them into a pit dug for their reception, in St. Margaret's churchyard, close by.

Dean left a widow and children. From the day of his death till that of his burial the Parliament allowed them £100 *per diem* in consideration of the very eminent services he had rendered to the Commonwealth.

For many additional particulars (omitted for want of space), see "Supplement to Leeds Worthies," pp. 551, 558,; [Col. Chester's "Westminster Abbey Registers," pp. 146-7; and the "Life of Richard Deane (the Regicide), Major-General and General at Sea," by the Rev. J. B. Deane, M.A., F.S.A., Rector of St. Martin Outwich, London, with two portraits, &c., 1871, Longmans & Co.

Richmond.   R. V. Taylor, B.A.

WILLIAM ETTY

HERE is an indefinable charm about true greatness that associates itself even with the inanimate objects by which it was surrounded in life. Hence we make pilgrimages to the homes and haunts and tombs of those who have gone before us, and have left enduring monuments of their undying mental powers for our behoof, gratification, or improvement. Many weary miles have been travelled for this gratification; and that it is a great one few can doubt, who have visited in a loving spirit the birth-place or grave of a Shakspere or a Raffaelle. But minor men share in a minor degree this art-worship, and few Englishmen will fail to take an interest in the memorials that the time - honoured city of York afford of our English Titian — William Etty. Etty published some years ago in the *Art-Journal* a charming piece of autobiography, having all the simplicity and freshness that such biography only retains. He notes there his great regard for his native city. He says—

William Etty, R.A.

"Like my favourite hero, Robinson Crusoe, I was born in the city of York—so he says, so say I; only he was born in 1632, I in 1787, March 10, of an honest and industrious family. Like Rembrandt and Constable, my father also was a miller, and his mill was standing, till this year, on the old York Road to London, about half a mile from York. My first panels on which I drew were the boards of my father's shop-floor, my first crayon a farthing's worth of white chalk."

This he wrote in the house depicted in our engraving. During all his wanderings his heart was in Yorkshire, and he went back to live and die in the historic city he loved so well.

The visitor to York who would desire a ready clue through its labyrinthine streets to the retired nook where the last home of Etty

Etty's House.

still stands, should pass the ferry from the railway station, and take the road opposite the gate of the Museum gardens; it leads direct to Coney Street: a short distance down this street there stands, on the right hand, the Church of St. Martin, a decorative piece of architecture, to which the attention is at once directed by one of those projecting clocks, a reigning favourite with our great-grandfathers. This is supported by massive ironwork, formed into foliage and flowers, and possessing more claim to attention on the score of artistic excellence than is usual in such works. It is surmounted by a quaint figure of a naval officer, in the costume of Queen Anne's era, using an astrolabe. Turning into the small square which is beside this church, we see in front a cottage residence, with heavy carved door, solid window frames, and a deeply-pitched roof. It may have been the parsonage house at one period; it seems fitted for the Dr. Primrose of Goldsmith's immortal story. It is, however, the house in which Etty lived and died. Shortly before his death he had attended the funeral of a friend in the churchyard of St. Olave, and he then desired to be buried in that spot provided he died in York; both events happened, and we will retrace our steps to visit the last resting-place of the painter: few lie in a more picturesque locality.

The churchyard of St. Olave adjoins the beautiful grounds of the Yorkshire Philosophical Society, where one of the most interesting local museums in the kingdom is situated, as well as fragments of ancient buildings, including a portion of the Roman wall of the city of York; the noble multangular tower, one of its defences, and the elegant

ruins of the Benedictine Abbey of St. Mary. The original foundation of this once large and opulent religious house was prior to the Norman Conquest; the ruins we now look upon are the remains of the work of the Abbot Simon de Warwick, completed in the latter half of the thirteenth century, the Augustan age of Gothic architecture in England, when it exhibited the chastest proportion and the most elegant conception, combined with an amount of decorative enrichment controlled by the truest taste. These walls, beautiful in decay, bound the churchyard of St. Olave, the church being partly constructed of its

Etty's Tomb.

stones; a series of arcades occupy the lower portion of the walls, and about their centre is a pointed arch, once acting as the northern entrance to the choir. This arch was closed, but was opened that the tomb of Etty might be seen from the grounds. This tomb stands exactly opposite the arch, and is slightly orna-

C

39

mented with Gothic panels and quatrefoils, forming a frame to the simple inscription—

"WILLIAM ETTY, ROYAL ACADEMICIAN."

Trees wave over it and peep beneath the arch; no fitter "framework" could have been desired for a painter's tomb; few have one in a more picturesque locality, fewer still have been thus publicly honoured by their fellow-townsmen as Etty has been by the men of York. They are "honoured in honouring him," and it is pleasant that this true aphorism is now more generally felt in England than it used to be. William Etty died on the 13th of November, 1849.

London.   F. W. FAIRHOLT, F.S.A.

WILLIAM P FRITH

WILLIAM POWELL FRITH, R.A., was born at Studley, near Ripon, in Yorkshire, in 1819. Evincing an early bias for art, he was placed at Mr. Sass's drawing school in 1835, and in 1837 became a student of the Royal Academy. In 1839 he exhibited his first picture at the British Institution, being the head of one of Mr. Sass's children. In 1840 his picture of "Malvolio before the Countess Olivia," exhibited at the Royal Academy, gained great applause. Five years later, his "Village Pastor," a scene drawn from Goldsmith, raised him, not only into notice, but to fame; and obtained for him his election as an Associate of the Royal Academy. This picture has been engraved by Holl. He had previously exhibited, with considerable success, a variety of works evincing steady progress, and among which we may mention "The Parting Interview of Leicester and the Countess Amy;" a scene from the "Vicar of Wakefield," called "Measuring Heights," in illustration of the passage: "My wife would have both stand up to see which was the tallest;" a capital subject from "The Merry Wives of Windsor;" and a picture of "John Knox and Mary Queen of Scots." In 1846 he painted a companion picture to the "Village Pastor," "The Return from Labour," and a humorous episode from the "Bourgeois Gentilhomme." His "English Merry-Making a Hundred Years Ago," exhibited in 1847, was full of picturesque beauty and graphic humour, and has been engraved for the London Art Union. Then followed, in 1848, "The Peasant Girl Accused of Witchcraft;" in 1849, "The Coming of Age," a pleasing tableau of Elizabethan manners, which has since been engraved; in 1850, "Sancho and the Duchess;" in 1851, "Hogarth at Calais;" and in 1852, "Pope Making Love to Lady Wortley Montague." In 1853 Mr. Frith was elected a Royal Academician. In 1854, a picture painted with consummate ability, entitled, "Life at the Seaside," showed that he was determined no more to recur to threadbare subjects, drawn from novels, but to fill his portfolio with sketches of the real men and women of the time. The

"Derby Day," exhibited in 1858, produced a still greater and more lasting sensation. In 1859 he exhibited "Charles Dickens in his Study," and in 1860 "Claude Duval, the Highwayman, compelling a

Lady to Dance with him." In 1862, after two years' labour, he completed "The Railway Station," a large picture, commissioned for the joint purpose of exhibition and engraving by Mr. Flatou, an enterprising

picture-dealer who, after exhibiting it for a London season, sold it, with his list of subscribers for the proposed engraving, to Mr. Graves, for £16,000. Since then Mr. Frith has received a commission from Her Majesty for a picture of the marriage of H.R.H. the Prince of Wales, for which he is to receive 3,000 guineas, besides 5,000 guineas from Mr. Flatou for the copyright. He has also received a commission from Mr. Gambart, another of our commercial patrons of art, for an elaborate picture of London Life. His two most remarkable recent works are "The Road to Ruin" and "The Race for Wealth," in which his power of rendering elaborate detail, with due regard to the distribution of light and shade, is prominently displayed.

London.   HENRY OTTLEY.

THOMAS CRESWICK

ONE of our most thoroughly national and popular landscape painters, was born at Sheffield in 1811. His favourite subjects—the wooded glens, tranquil rivers, and sunny pastures of his native land—are painted with sympathetic feeling. In the treatment of foliage he is peculiarly happy, and his aerial perspective is delicate and truthful, but his pictures, especially in his later period, lack warmth of colour. Amongst his numerous characteristic works are "England," "Passing Showers," "Old Trees," "Changeable Weather," "The Pathway to the Village Church," "A Summer's Afternoon," and "Home by the Sands." Creswick was elected a Royal Academician in 1851, and died in 1869.

London.   G. H. SHEPHERD.

JOHN HARLAND

JOHN HARLAND, says the Rev. Brooke Herford, "whose great-grandfather was an enterprising farmer and grazier, living near Dunkeld in the middle of the last century, was born at Hull, May 27, 1806." He was the eldest child of John Harland and his wife Mary, daughter of John Breasley of Selby. His father followed the combined businesses of clock and watch maker, and jeweller, in Scale Lane, Hull; and issued a medal in commemoration of the peace and end of the war in December, 1813. At the age of fourteen the boy went, on trial, into the office of Messrs. Allanson & Sydney, the proprietors of the *Hull Packet* newspaper, and was apprenticed to them for seven years from January 1, 1821, to learn letterpress printing. The celebrated painter Etty was Mr. Harland's predecessor as an apprentice; and when he removed from Hull to London he left a scrap-book, containing a series of early sketches, as a memento, in the hands of Mr. George Walker, a journeyman printer in the same office. "From the beginning of his apprenticeship he gave all his energies to self-improvement; soon rose from compositor to reader; then was put into the office; and, teaching himself short-hand, was advanced to reporting. With indomitable industry, he made for himself, during 1825-6, a system of short-hand in which he embodied all the best points of several stenographic systems, and soon became the most expert short-hand writer in the kingdom."

Mr. Harland continued as reporter and contributor to the Hull newspapers for several years after the expiration of his apprenticeship. During this period his reports were so remarkable for their fulness and accuracy, that they attracted the attention of every public speaker who visited the town. On one occasion he presented the Rev. Dr. Beard with so accurate a report of his address in Bond Alley Lane Chapel, that "he mentioned the circumstance to the late John Edward Taylor, who was then conducting the *Manchester Guardian* with that energy and ability which placed it at the head of the provincial press. The consequence was an offer which induced Mr. Harland to remove to

43

Manchester in November, 1830," in which city and its vicinity he resided till his death.

At first the *Guardian* was only a weekly paper ; but it began to be published on Wednesdays and Saturdays in 1836, and became a daily paper in 1855. Mr. Harland continued to occupy an important position on the staff through all these changes ; conducting the literary department of the journal with rare skill and industry, until July 1, 1839, when he was admitted to a partnership in the paper, which he retained till his retirement in December, 1860. " While thus busied with his own professional work, however, he found time for the cultivation of literary tastes in other and higher directions. Possessing a keen sense of humour ; endowed with considerable poetic powers ; skilled in mediæval Latin ; and a loving student of early English history, he speedily made himself a reputation among local literary men, and, as his pursuits took more decidedly the direction of archæology, gradually became widely known as an antiquary." He published many of his early dissertations in the columns of the *Guardian ;* some of which were afterwards included in the " Collectanea," issued by the Chetham Society, and other works. In December, 1854, he was elected a Fellow of the Society of Antiquaries, and was placed upon the Council of the Chetham Society in 1855 ; an office which he only vacated by death. He was also a member of the Historic Society of Lancashire and Cheshire ; to whose *Transactions* he contributed some interesting papers, and presented to their library a valuable series of antiquarian cuttings from the *Manchester Guardian.* To *Notes and Queries* Mr. Harland was an occasional contributor ; he supplied most of the articles relating to Lancashire to Chambers's " Book of Days ; " of which his accounts of " John Shaw's Club," and the " Rev. Joshua Brookes," may be particularised. In 1851 he published a series of " Ancient Charters and other Muniments of the Borough of Clithero ; " several of which were afterwards included in his " Mamecestre," and in the same year he printed the " Autobiography of William Stout, of Lancaster, wholesale and retail grocer and ironmonger, a member of the Society of Friends, A.D., 1665-1732." This quaint and characteristic work was dedicated to his friend A. B. Rowley, Esq., the owner of the manuscript, and several curious notes were added by Mr. Harland in illustration of portions of the text. Mr. Harland published " An Historical Account of Salley Abbey," in Yorkshire, during 1853, illustrated by a series of lithographic sketches of the existing remains. This work was appropriately dedicated to Dixon Robinson, Esq., of Clitheroe Castle, who largely promoted the publication. It contains by far the most accurate and complete account of these interesting ruins. To the *Reliquary* he contributed a paper on " Local and other Names and Words."

In 1864-5 he edited two volumes of "Court Leet Records" of the manor of Manchester. They contain many valuable accounts of the social and civil life of the inhabitants of that city during the sixteenth century. His introduction, preparatory chapter, notes and appendices, are especially curious and interesting. He closed his extracts at the date of the death of Queen Elizabeth; and expressed a hope that other extracts would be made commencing with the reign of James I. This hope was not realised. During Mr. Harland's connection with the *Manchester Guardian* he published in that journal, and in the *Weekly Express*, a vast number of antiquarian articles of much local interest. A selection from these was issued in two volumes as "Collectanea relating to Manchester and its neighbourhood at various periods."

The last and greatest work he undertook was a new edition of Baines's "History of Lancashire." It was originally issued in four volumes, and had long been out of print. When it was decided to republish the work it was deemed advisable to issue it in two volumes; and although the labour of verification and completion approached at times to a re-writing of large portions of the book, Mr. Harland did not shrink from the task, and he did his work well. The writer visited him towards the close of 1867, and found him hard at work with the last sheets of the first volume. He was then looking haggard and careworn—the heavy work was evidently telling on his constitution; and yet both in conversation with myself, and in his letters to Mr. Gent, joint publisher of this and several of his other works, he spoke and wrote hopefully of completing his labours within a reasonable time. On my next visit I found he was seriously ill. His medical attendant durst not risk the excitement of an interview, and I left without seeing him. In two days more he had passed to his rest. He died on the 23rd April, 1868, and his remains were interred in Rusholme Road Cemetery the Tuesday following.

Mr. Harland "was twice married; first in 1833 to Mary, daughter of the late Samuel Whitfield, of Birmingham, who died in 1849; secondly, in 1852, to Eliza, daughter of the late Joseph Pilkington, of Manchester, who, together with four children by the first marriage, and five by the second, survives him. By a wide circle of friends he was warmly esteemed as a kind and genial friend; a sincere and single-minded Christian. Born a Churchman, he became a Unitarian by conviction in 1828. In the busiest year of his newspaper life, when he might have claimed exemption from extra work, he found time to be teacher and superintendent in a Sunday-school; and throughout his life was as active as he was unobtrusive in doing good." Such is the just and well-deserved tribute paid to his memory by the Rev. Brooke Herford, who carried on and completed the "History of Lancashire" with competent ability and in the spirit of his predecessor. Mr. Harland's collection of works on short-hand was very extensive, ranging from the sixteenth century downwards. They are now in the Chetham Library as a permanent memorial of one whose literary life was so intimately associated with the varied stores contained in those quaint old rooms.

Burnley.   *The late* T. T. WILKINSON.

CHARLOTTE BRONTË

THE story of Charlotte Brontë's life is one of the most fascinating in our language. The author of "Jane Eyre" was a mere reed, physically—a woman frail, yet strong; spiritual, yet still indomitable. She had a rare and unusual development, and her domestic life was one of the most singular ever known. She was born at Thornton, in the West Riding, the 21st day of April, 1816, and was the third of six children. . Her father, Patrick Brontë, was for more than forty years incumbent of Haworth, and the solitude of the grey old parsonage at that place nursed her imaginative faculty, and in the absolute dearth of society she learned to think and to write. She lost her mother when she was five years old, and was left the care-taker of her younger sisters and brother, after the two eldest sisters had been sent to school. Mr. Brontë did not known how to undertake the care and education of so many children, but he was a student himself, and enforced his spartan ideas of study upon his willing pupils. Fortunately they were all the inheritors of his intellectual tastes, and to this circumstance they owed all the pleasure they enjoyed. After the death of her mother, the two sisters older than Charlotte were put to a school kept for clergymen's daughters, and later, Charlotte and Emily were sent to join them. These two sisters both died from the treatment they received at this school, and it would have ended the lives of the younger girls if they had not been recalled. As it was, their health was permanently injured, and Charlotte, to the latest day of her life, had cause to remember it. She never grew an inch in stature after leaving this school

G. Richmond. del.   J.C. Armytage. sc.

Sincerely yours
C Brontë

Published by Smith, Elder & Cº 15, Waterloo Place. London.

She was the smallest of women, and attributed all her physical woes to the treatment she had received there.

She remained at home from this time, taking the responsibility of caring for the three younger children, and dividing her time between her books and their comfort. Her absorbing occupation when free to engage in it was writing, and her purely imaginative composition at this time was precocious and singular, while the amount produced was immense. Her life was largely influenced by that of her more masculine sister Emily, who, if she had lived, would have been the greatest, though perhaps not the more successful, author of the two. Bramwell, the golden-haired idol of the home, and Anne, the youngest of that

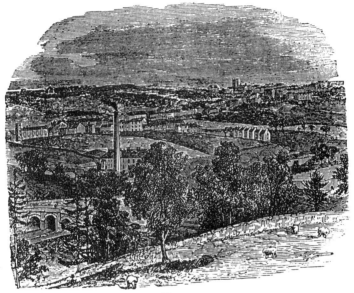

Haworth.

family, were both full of promise, and the eldest sister looked upon herself as the least among them all. She was the plainest in personal appearance, yet so spiritual and refined in organisation was she, that the expression of her face was a study to her home companions, and a marvel to those who could not know that a great soul was enshrined in her little body. Charlotte was now sixteen years of age, but she was so small, that she called herself stunted, but she was well formed, and as a child exquisitely refined. In her attire she was neat and dainty, though her clothing, as befitted her father's idea of a minister's daughter, was plain and homely.

Her head was beautifully shaped, and very large, while her great brown eyes beamed with animation. Her hands were peculiar in their formation, and her fingers had a fineness of sensation and a restless motion arising from the extreme sensibility of her organism. They were never still, and unconsciously she would clinch them together with a force that left a bruised scar for days. Having a finely shaped head, she had a broad and handsome brow, and in her day it was not considered fashionable to hide it. Charlotte Bronté as a girl of nineteen had much book knowledge of a desultory kind, but her definite acquirements were few. She was not very reliable in orthodox matters; of religion in its sunny aspect and beautifying influences she knew little, and it was not surprising that she early exhibited antagonistic feelings towards the calvinistic views of her father, and hated with girlish viru the long-faced curates and travelling preachers who occasionally appeared at the parsonage table.

Charlotte Bronté loved music, and its influence over her was powerful. It was a passion with her, and her soul, responsive to melody, caught the refrain of every accent of softness or sweetness, and its influence reached the world in the heart-music she sang, which vibrates and reverberates wherever the Anglo-Saxon tongue is known !

There is something fascinating in the pictures given of Haworth parsonage at this early stage of her career. Haworth is a sombre place, and its people retain now the dialect which Charlotte depicted so successfully in " Shirley." The straggling village has but one street, and the old grey stone parsonage stands quite at the top of the hill, facing down it, and surrounded on all sides but one by the village graveyard. The view from the side where there are no graves is the bleakest one of all. It looks out upon moors which are as barren as a prairie in winter, and as colourless as a desert in summer. But the changeless monotony of these moors grated not at all harshly on the girls of a home that was even more cheerless, and they spent some of their happiest hours upon them. A walk in the dull and waning light of a winter's afternoon, enabled these lonely children to return to their writing at eveningtide with new zeal, and while the wind sang its requiem without, they wrote their weird and extraordinary compositions.

It was the custom of the sisters when at home, to sew at night until nine o'clock, when their father usually retired, and they then spent the interval before retiring to rest in talking over past cares and troubles, in planning for the future, and consulting each other as to their aspirations. This night time in the kitchen in after years was spent in discussing the plots of their novels. Charlotte, and indeed the others, had written much that was tolerably successful even in their own opinion, and for advice and counsel Charlotte wrote to Southey. He replied graciously, and was evidently interested in the young girl, for he invited her to visit him at the " Lakes." But there was no money in that home to devote to visiting, and Charlotte and Emily had both concluded that their writings would not bring it to them. Charlotte proposed to Emily the idea of enlarging the parsonage and opening a school there, and Emily, who had tried to be a governess with even less success than Charlotte, gladly assented to this plan that would enable them to live at home and together. The obstacle they had to contend against was their lack of accomplishments, and they resolved to conquer this drawback. To do it successfully they went to Brussels to study for six months. Charlotte was twenty-six years old then. At the expiration of the six months the two sisters were offered positions in the school, and Charlotte accepted the offer, Emily returning home. This step in her life was a mistake. It has left her fame and honour as a woman bright as sunshine, but it was here that Charlotte Bronté

Haworth Parsonage.

ceased to be a girl, and came, through a baptism of pain, to her true status as a woman. Her staying in Brussels was an unreasonable impulse, and for her selfish folly she suffered, as she herself has said, a withdrawal for more than two years of happiness and peace of mind. Her heart had been captured by an acquaintance in Brussels, and Paul Emanuel, the hero of "Villette," was the portraiture of the man she loved. Every word of that book is a veritable history, a literal transcription of actual facts. She was the one English girl in a house full of French-speaking people, and the man she loved was an inmate of that school. None ever knew from her what she suffered in her unfortunate attachment for the relative of her employer—a cruel despotic woman, who is described accurately in "Villette"—but they realised a depth and strength of character not before observable. Charlotte Bronté learned herself through a great tempest of love that swept over her life, a tempest which she was enabled by her native purity, strong character, and excellent discipline, to master. She had walked quite up to temptation's mouth, and then walked away, a nobler woman for ever after. Had she not known the experience she did, we should not have such books as she wrote, for no woman without actual self-knowledge could ever have pictured such a character as Rochester or been able to write such a book as "Jane Eyre." When Charlotte reached home from Brussels, she showed Emily and Anne some of the poetry she had been writing of late, and was greatly surprised to learn that they too had tried their talents in that direction. They consulted together and ventured to publish their compositions. Charlotte wrote to a London publisher, and an agreement was made by which the book was issued at their expense. It was called "Poems of Currer, Ellis, and Acton Bell," and, it is needless to add, it had no success.

The year 1846 was one of peculiar domestic hardships and unusual mental activity to Charlotte Bronté. She had a troubled heart to cure and an increased necessity for work that would pay her. She accompanied her father, at this time, to Manchester to have an operation performed upon his eyes, and while in a strange city and amid strangers she made another attempt at book-making. Previous to this time she had written the "Professor," a story which no publisher would accept. With the soiled manuscript of this first attempt now before her, with the memory of her home, and the thought of her dissipated brother whose dark shadow rested over it; in the presence of her fault-finding father, and dwelling constantly upon her absent sisters, whom she loved so truly, she began "Jane Eyre." It was under such circumstances that her great talent burst forth, asserted its sway, and made her more contented and happy, for her imaginative faculty was, under all circum-stances, a source of comfort. Think of it—ye who wait for opportunities instead of making them—and appreciate as it deserves to be appreciated, the brave woman who could work even under such circumstances.

Charlotte published her book under the masculine *nom de plume*, "Currer Bell," and told no one but her sisters of its existence. When it was published, and before it had raised the storm of applause that followed its public reception, she took a copy of it in one hand and an adverse review of it in the other to her father, and quietly told him of her task and the result. Then for the first time he realised what the postman's call meant when some time before he had stopped at the door with a letter for Currer Bell, and was met with the reply from himself that there was no such person in the village.

Then came the abuse which the critics, who could not appreciate her book, heaped upon it. She was assaulted as the exponent of views not compatible with womanly purity, and her great soul was inexpressibly pained

The quiet home-life at the parsonage was continued after the publication of "Jane Eyre," and Charlotte and her sisters had their hands full in watching over their ruined brother, and cheer as best they could their disappointed and unhappy father. "Shirley," the second of her novels was commenced and brought out in the midst of fearful domestic anguish. When Charlotte was thirty-five years old she began to write her last work, "Villette." It was her beloved brain-child, far dearer to her than her powerful "Shirley," in which is so graphically pourtrayed the character of Emily as the heroine, or her more popular "Jane Eyre." Every sentence of "Villette" was written literally through her tears. The task was a cruel, if a passionately absorbing one. She was painting the darkest chapter of

Haworth Church.

her own life and suffering, the loneliness of death in a house where the great destroyer had been so persistent.

One of the least known incidents in the life of Charlotte Brontë is that of her marriage. Among the few of her father's acquaintances whom she knew well was Mr. Nicholls, his curate, who had been living at Haworth some years when he asked her to become his wife. When she told her father of the honour that had been paid her, and asked his advice, to her astonishment he grew violently angry; denounced his assistant as presumptuous, and was so unreasonable that Charlotte made haste to assure him of her willingness to decline the offer. In course of time, however, he relented, and proposed to re-call Mr. Nicholls, who had left Haworth, and asked his daughter to write him. The result was, that very quietly one bright June morning in 1854 she became Charlotte Nicholls. She entered into her husband's interests and occupation as much as she could, but she was clearly unfitted for an active, matter-of-fact existence. When the new year came it found her fast on her last journey. She died very quietly one Saturday morning in March, 1855, in the eighth month after her marriage, and the ninth year of her authorship. "The solemn tolling of Haworth Church bell spoke forth the fact of her death to the villagers who had known her from a child, and whose hearts shivered within them as they thought of the two (father and husband) sitting desolate and alone in the old grey house."

All that is left of the Brontés in Haworth are the graves in the now renovated church and their memory, kept green by the thousands who have flocked there to learn all the particulars of the life of the woman who had made her name a familiar one to the reading world.

Of all the women of England of the present century, the two who may be ranked as Charlotte Bronté's worthiest successors, as writers, are Mrs. Browning and George Eliot. The life-histories of both these women are of equal interest with their authorship. No one thinks of Mrs. Browning without recalling her invalidism, and her happy wifehood and motherhood. None now think of George Eliot without a feeling of pride in her as the largest endowed woman of this age, and one of the most exalted in her domestic life and affectionate nature.

Charlotte Bronté had more natural talent than either Mrs. Browning or George Eliot; she had far less culture than either, and a more limited acquaintance with the world. But she was the completest woman of her era, the worthy predecessor in authorship of these two great women. Neither of them has given to the world more than did Charlotte Bronté. She gave her sister women the inheritance of her life—womanly excellence, literary greatness, noble characteristics, and a stainless history.

Her fame and her glory belong to no land or country, while her memory is cherished by the cultured of every clime. The remembrance of her life is an inspiration to all who, like her, have pressed their bleeding feet upon the hard rocks of life, and left their impress upon them.

Nearly three decades of time have glided into the unreturning past since the mural which bears her name was placed in Haworth Church. There now rests all that is earthly of that wondrous woman whose name touches a tender chord in the hearts of millions. All over the world her name is venerated. Inasmuch as she used every atom of available power, her life was truly heroic, and when all the battles of intellect are recorded, inscribed high upon the scroll of fame will appear the imperishable name of Charlotte Bronté.

Philadelphia.   LAURA C. HOLLOWAY.

JOHN JAMES

John James, F.S.A., was born at the village of West Witton, on the 22nd of January, 1811, and received the first rudiments of his education in the village school of the place. So reluctant was he, that he had often to be forced to go to school by his mother, who became a widow when he was about three years old. That he loved to play truant can hardly be wondered at, when we remember that West Witton, Wensleydale, is situated on the south bank of the river Yore, and overlooks some of the most beautiful scenery in Yorkshire. Bolton Castle, and the charming park and hall, where Lord Bolton resides, are in close proximity His mother, after the death of her first husband, John James, married one John Wilson, but she also out-lived him, and died in 1853, at the age of 88 years. Her father, a Mr. Glasby, died in 1813, aged 95. Her second husband died at the age of 73 ; such is the length of life in Wensleydale. I will here mention a curious circumstance relating to this John Glasby. When he was 80 years old, concluding that he could not live much longer, he had his coffin made, and kept it in his house beside him for the remainder of his life, fifteen years, when he died, and was buried in it

Although young John was so averse to learning in his boyhood, he soon took to it eagerly, and with the help of a young comrade, one Ralph Tomlinson, a schoolmaster, he soon became proficient ; and about this time he began to work at a lime-kiln for tenpence a day, which was all spent in books. Through the interest of a gentleman of West Witton, a Mr. Anderson, he became a clerk in the office of the late Ottiwell Tomlin, Solicitor, of Richmond, who is buried at West Witton Church. On leaving Mr. Tomlin he went to London, but not being successful he removed to the law office of the late Mr. Tolson, of Bradford, where he remained until the death of Mr. Tolson. His employer treated him with great consideration and kindness, and encouraged him in his literary efforts ; and it was during his connection with Mr. Tolson that he compiled the materials for the *History of Bradford*, and which he published in 1842.

The literary advantages of Bradford were then very scanty, and for the most part out of the reach of an obscure lawyer's clerk ; but such as they were Mr. James made good use of them. He became correspondent of the *York Herald* newspaper, and sought out the society of men with literary proclivities, and by this means gathered as well as communicated knowledge. The Mechanics' Institute had been formed some years, he early joined it, and became a member of the committee. He was also one of a small debating club which had a short but vigorous life ; and from the commencement of the *Bradford Observer*, in 1834, he was an occasional contributor to its columns. Indeed his first efforts at composition are to be found in its earlier issues. He had the chance of becoming a lawyer, but, though gifted with a wonderful faculty for research, his tastes led him into the pleasanter paths of literature, and I believe that he never regretted that he had given himself up to the muses. I have seen some of his compositions in rhyme, which were creditable, but he early showed his good sense by confining himself to prose, which was indeed elegant.

His next work was writing a memoir of John Nicholson, commonly called the " Airedale Poet," and this was prefixed to an edition of the poet's works. Into this task he would seem to have thrown his whole soul, for as a biography, it is all that can be desired.

Then followed the " History of the Worsted Manufacture in England," a work of immense research, and which is now hardly obtainable. It contains four plates, illustrating the worsted processes in manufacture, besides views engraved on steel of Bradford, Saltaire, Halifax, and Dean Clough, all paid for by the late Sir Titus Salt, Bart.; the late Joseph Crossley, Esq., and others. At a meeting of the British Association in Leeds, he read a paper on the " Statistics of Trade in Yorkshire." This was the cause of his being personally introduced to the present Sir Edward Baines, then M.P. for Leeds. Soon after this the Messrs. Black, of Edinburgh, wrote to Mr. Baines, wishing him to point out some one qualified to write an article for them on Yorkshire. Mr. Baines pointed out Mr. James as the most likely person. He then wrote it, and it appeared in the *Encyclopædia Britannica*, for which he received seven guineas. In 1862, he wrote some papers for the *Bradford Observer* from the Exhibition then being held in London, on the exhibits of Bradford and the neighbourhood. When his old friend the late Mr. Robert Story, formerly of Gargrave, died, he wrote a memoir of him, and it was appended to an edition of his poems printed for the benefit of his widow. He also gave a lecture in the Huddersfield Philosophical Hall, on the " Philosophy of Lord Bacon and the systems which preceded it ;" and this was also published in a pamphlet. In 1863, Thomas Wright, Esq., F.S.A., of London, read a paper before the Archæological Association, then at Leeds, written by Mr. James, entitled " On the Little British Kingdom of Elmete," and which I inserted in *Collectanea Bradfordiana*. He then set to work on the *continuation* of his History of Bradford, and this was published in 1866. This work embodies the labours and research of Mr. James's later and riper years, and is a monument of his industry.

He now went to reside with his old friend Mr. Edward Collinson, at Netheredge, Sheffield ; but he was a frequent visitor to Bradford, where he was highly esteemed. His reputation as an author was deservedly high, and I never met with a man who had a more thorough knowledge of the manifold beauties of our county, or who had accquired such a general information of its varied interests. His fame had spread far and wide, so that even on his death-bed, a letter was received from the Messrs. Chambers, of Edinburgh, asking him to write for them a paper on " Yorkshire," for their Encyclopædia, then in course of publication. The request came too late to receive attention.

Stern death which comes alike to all, came at length to him. He was struck with paralysis of the right side, and became speechless, and after lying thus for seven weeks, with a patience truly wonderful, he expired in his own villa residence, at Netheredge, Sheffield, on Thursday, July 4th, 1867. His body was removed on Monday, the 8th, to Leyburn, and his funeral took place at West Witton Church, the same afternoon. The town of Sheffield was represented by his god-son, John James Collinson, and Bradford by his friend and fellow-labourer, the writer of this notice. He left all his real estate to his cousin, Abram James, deceased, whose heir is John James, of West Witton.

Mr. James lived and died a bachelor. This is the more to be regretted as he was so loveable a man. Young children, grown men, and maidens, and even garrulous old age, were alike delighted with his company and conversation. As an antiquary he was indefatigable. As a friend he was ever firm and true. Thoroughly conscientious himself, he could not bear the want of it in others, and his geniality won him troops of friends. But he is gone! And "he shall return to his house no more, neither shall his place know him any more." His name, however, is bound up with the history of the town and trade of Bradford, and will endure as long.

Ship'ey. ABRAHAM HOLROYD.

DR JOHN FOTHERGILL

THE earliest time at which the name of Fothergill occurs in history is, so far as I have been able to trace, in connection with the siege of York by the Norman William.

Old Drake, in his celebrated "Eboracum," gives an amusing account of an adventure in which the Conqueror and his knight Fothergill were concerned, which led to the capture of the "Noble old Citty," and which briefly may be related as follows :—

"The North Riding and the City of York having long withstood the efforts to conquer them, Duke William determined himself to lay siege to the city, which he commenced on St. Thomas's Day. Retiring in the evening, after an unsuccessful day, to his camp at Skelton, he met two friars, and on inquiring where they dwelt, they said at York, and were of a poore Priory of St. Peter's, and had been to obtain 'some relief to their fellows against Christmas.' One of them was laden with a wallett of victuals and a shoulder of mutton in his hand, and two great cakes hung about his necke, one of backe and another of his breast. The other had a bottle of ale and a wallet filled with beef and mutton.

---

* For the loan of the excellent engravings which accompany this sketch, we are indebted to the kindness of the Centenary Committee of Ackworth School. Of the portrait of Dr. Fothergill, the art critic, John Ruskin, says :—"Quite splendid drawing and woodcutting." The same authority says of the View of Carr End :—"This plate is quite uniquely beautiful, so far as my knowledge reaches, in expressing the general character of Old Yorkshire "

" The Normans did confer with these poore friars, and promised them large gifts if so they would let them into their monastery, and also give them money. The Conqueror also promised that he would make their Priory all new, and give them great revenue, which he did after perform. Soe they did condescend to let them into the Citty at a postern gate; and the King sent for his army, and he, with his general of the field, Fothergill, took the Citty that night."

The Conqueror acted well to Sir Robert Clifford and others, who had so nobly defended their ancient city, " and willed that they should ask what they would have, and they should have it."

"They demanded of him if they might have every St. Thomas's day a Friar of St. Peter's Priory, painted like a Jew, to ride of a horse, with the taile in one hand and shoulder of Mutton in the other, with a cake before his breast and another at his backe, all throughout the citty, and the boyes of the citty to ride with him, and proclaim that the citty was taken that day through the treachery of the Friars; which it is added was continued as a memorial to that day."

This Knight Fothergill married " the faire Isabel Poulton," or Boulton, who had as dower many Manors, including, among others, those of " Sedber and Garsdale."

That the Fothergill family known to us were descendants of the Norman Baron and the " faire Isabel " we do not pretend to say; but this can easily be traced—that for three or four centuries, families of this name have resided in the wild and secluded valleys of Ravenstone-dale and Mallerstang, both valleys in Westmoreland, which adjoin upon " Sedber and Wensleydale." Sufficient for us, for the purpose of this sketch, is the fact, that a John Fothergill migrated thence to Counter-set in Wensleydale, and afterwards to Carr End soon after the year 1600.

The simple humble life of the " Statesman " or " Dalesman " of Yorkshire or Westmoreland, as it existed centuries ago, does not present many incidents for the historian to dwell upon, and thus it is that until the rise of Quakerism we know comparatively little of the ancestors of Dr. Fothergill's family, except that they had undoubtedly dwelt in these vales for many previous generations.

But Quaker history—which has preserved for us, like " flies in amber," lives or notices of so large a number of its earliest members— tells us that at Carr End, on the banks of the small and quiet lake of " Semer Water," there dwelt Alexander and Ann Fothergill, who were probably convinced by George Fox (about the year 1652), as " he passed up the Dales warning people to fear God, and preaching tho everlasting Gospel to them."* Here,. in 1676, John Fothergill the elder, the father of Dr. Fothergill was born.

He appears to have inherited the little estate at Carr End after the death of his father, in 1695, who had suffered much the previous year from months of imprisonment in York for refusing to pay tithes, in company with many of our ancestors.

---

* George Fox's Journal, folio, p 72.

John Fothergill.

When about thirty-four he married Margaret Hough, of Sutton, in Cheshire, a woman likeminded with himself, and settled down for some years in the old family house.

John Fothergill, the future doctor, was born on the 8th of March, 1712. In very early life he was placed under the care of his mother's family, the Houghs of Cheshire, and after leaving the elementary day school at Frodsham, in Cheshire, he was sent (at twelve) to the old-established Grammar School, of about 120 boys, at Sedbergh, on the borders of Yorkshire and Westmoreland, and not very far from his father's house. There he seems to have remained for four years, and obtained that thorough education which was of such good service in after life. Dr. Saunders was the head master at this time.

Leaving Sedbergh School in 1728, at the age of sixteen he was apprenticed for seven years (as the Indenture, still in existence, proves) to Benjamin Bartlett, an eminent apothecary at Bradford.

It was probably as some recognition of the fidelity of his services that he was liberated before the expiration of the term of his apprenticeship, to pursue his medical studies in Edinburgh, which from the eminence of the men who at that period filled the Professors' chairs, had the highest repute ; suffice it to name—Drs. Munro, Alston, and Rutherford, all of them pupils of the celebrated Boerhaave, of Leyden.

His first visit to London was probably made during the summer recess of 1735, as we find an entry of, " Paid my freight from Leith by vessel to London £1 11s. 6d.," a voyage which appears to have taken as long a period as is now occupied by the steamers between Liverpool and New York; the voyage to London taking nine days and to return to Edinburgh even a longer period.

The 29th of October, 1736, saw Dr. Fothergill, at the age of twenty-four, in London, where, the more thoroughly to qualify himself for practice, he entered as a pupil at St. Thomas's Hospital. During this time, though chiefly thus occupied and in visiting the poor, he took a few fees, some at 10s. 6d., and others at 21s.

Fairly established in practice, he took a house in White Hart Court, Gracechurch Street (in 1740), adjoining the once well-known Friends' Meeting-house there. As appears from the little book, so often quoted, he received fees in this year to the amount of 105 guineas, and expended £104, of which £44 was spent in travelling in Holland and Germany for twelve weeks.

We have now brought the life of Dr. Fothergill to the period of his establishment as a physician in the City of London, what was then truly " *The City of London* " ; a London which, though then deemed " immense," had a population of scarcely three-quarters of a million.

Here, during the succeeding forty years, he laboured unremittingly, attaining to the highest rank in his profession, and numbering among his patients some of the most worthy and distinguished characters of the century. But in estimating his character it would be a great mistake to regard him simply as a great physician ; it was in its highest

Ackworth School.

(See Page 141.)

and widest meaning, *as a friend to man*, that he has a claim upon our regard and admiration. There is scarcely a point which affects the physical, moral, and religious interest of the race, which did not attract his attention, and receive benefit from his judicious and untiring labours.

After his father's death, the estate of Carr End, containing about 200 acres (then worth about £30 a year) went to the eldest son, who also practised as a lawyer ; and as the Doctor had only £60 as his share of the family property it is evident that Dr. F. was solely indebted to his own exertions for his position. Even this " Patter money," as his sister Ann calls it, he made over to her, adding £40 more of his own. Of Carr End and its surroundings, a few words may not unfitly be inserted here.

There is no need to say a word to Yorkshire readers in praise of Wensleydale, with its broad meadow slopes of luxuriant grass running up to the moorland heights above, or downward, amidst the most lovely fringes of trees broken by an occasional " scar " or cliff, to the peaceful river below. Semmerdale, situate at the head of the valley, is one of the numerous smaller valleys which run nearly at right angles with the larger vale of Wensley, and in which the little stream which flows from the heights above forms, before it enters the Ure, a little lake in the midst of bare, marshy meadows ; but the whole are surrounded by low mountainous hills, which give to it a sense of secluded beauty. Towards its southern end, about four miles from Askrigg, Carr End is situated on the rocky road which leads across the hills to Marsett or Kettlewell, at a point where it suddenly drops down nearly to a level with the lake The house is so shut out from the road by tall trees, and the rock at the foot of which it is built, that, though within a few yards, the traveller is scarcely aware of its existence until almost passed. The house, which faces nearly east, is on the edge of the low meadows which surround the lake, and from the little garden, once kept trim and neat, with its little lawn and flower-beds, but now chiefly devoted to potatoes, there are views both right and left, especially the former, worthy of the pencil of Dr. Fothergill's collateral descendant, the late George William Fothergill, whose death cut short a career of great artistic promise. Of the house at Carr End but little can be said. There is a stone let into the gateway by which you enter the garden, on which is carved " J. F., 1677," but the house is of a later period, and has a neglected, desolate air. The present tenant is a small farmer, and a part of the house is let off to the village schoolmaster ; as we saw it in the quiet, fading light of the evening, the plaintive cry of a plover, as it came to us from the moorland, seemed a fitting wail over the departed life of Carr End as it surrounded the boyish days of Dr. Fothergill. The estate passed away from the Fothergill family so recently as 1841.

Dr. Fothergill began during this period to publish in the *Gentleman's Magazine* a monthly report of the weather and temperature,

Carr End, Semerwater.

chiefly in relation to disease, and regularly continued it for several years (1751-6), when the press of his engagements, combined with other causes, compelled him to give up this most useful and very interesting work.

He may be said to have been the pioneer in the road to those meteorological observations which we all now consider so important. There was at this time no registration of deaths or births, and burials, and Dr. Fothergill used all his influence to effect this most desirable object ; but it was not until some years after his death that this was carried out, and the Bills of Mortality were reduced to a· system.

It was during this period (1754) that he was elected a Fellow of the College of Physicians of Edinburgh

John Wesley was one of his patients during this time ; but ill as he was, his earnest spirit did not allow him to carry out the Doctor's advice to rest and repair to the hot wells at Bristol for change. Probably, like his comrade Whitfield, he thought "that *perpetual preaching* was a better remedy than a perpetual blister."

In 1762 Dr. Fothergill purchased the gardens at Upton, so well known in after days as the hospitable residence and grounds of the late Samuel Gurney. It contained at that time a house, garden, and about thirty acres of land, afterwards increased to about sixty acres.

Dr. Fothergill frequently offered rewards for the introduction into this country, or the colonies, of plants of medicinal value. For instance, he offered a premium of £100 to two captains of ships for living plants of the Winter's Bark (*Cortex Winteranus*), a native of extra tropical South America, and named after Captain Winter, who used it as a remedy for scurvy.

Dr. Fothergill's love of botany brought him into correspondence with the celebrated Linnæus, and he not only generously helped, but superintended the great and expensive botanical work of John Millar, published to illustrate the Linnæan system. He also largely assisted the authors of other scientific books, as for example, Dr. Russell's " History of Aleppo " (afterwards writing a Memoir of Dr. Russell), and Dr. Cleghorn's " Diseases of Minorca ; " Edwards' beautiful work on the " Birds of Great Britain," and Drury's " Entomology," were largely assisted by him.

Nor must the munificent assistance which Dr. Fothergill rendered to Anthony Purver, in the translation and publication of his version of tho Old and New Testaments, be overlooked. Not only did he give pecuniary assistance, to the extent of £2,000, to the translator (a poor self-taught man), but, it is said, revised the whole of the sheets as they passed through the press, and subsequently did all in his power by recommendation or gift to promote the circulation of the folio.

Notwithstanding the intense pressure of his varied engagements, we find that he was an Elder, and became a Member of the Yearly Meeting's Committee, appointed to visit the Meetings of Friends in the various counties of England. He was thus engaged for many weeks, chiefly in Yorkshire, Lancashire, and Westmoreland, and it was whilst thus engaged that he paid his last visit to Carr End, in 1777.

It may have been that these visits, and the ignorance he found in many quarters, gave additional force to his long-cherished desire to see a sound and Christian education more generally valued, and made accessible to all classes in the Society of Friends. Be this as it may, it was in this year that he succeeded in giving a practical shape to his long-cherished wish; and we now come to that point in our narrative which, extending over the three remaining years of Dr. Fothergill's life, gives the History of the establishment of Ackworth School, which was, as Luke Howard justly called it, " The Era of a Reformation in our Religious Society."*

Nor does it render him less entitled to have his name handed down to the latest posterity as the founder of Ackworth School, that he did not, as has often been stated, purchase it wholly and present it to the Society. And jointly with his name, and entitled to our gratitude and remembrance, we must not omit to mention that of his warm and devoted friend David Barclay† (of London), and in Yorkshire, those of his friends, John Hustler (of Bradford), and William Tuke (of York).

In the summer of 1780 (the last of his life) Dr. Fothergill paid his second, and subsequently a third, visit to Ackworth School.

One of the most important objects of Dr. Fothergill's life was now accomplished, and we can only devote a few words to the account of its close. Before doing so, however, the following graphic description of Dr. Fothergill, as he appeared probably at the time of his last visit to York, written by a great-nephew, cannot fail to be of interest:—

Extract from Records of John Fothergill, of York (1793).

"Dr. Fothergill was pious, generous, and benevolent, rather above the middle age; very delicate and slender, of a sanguine temperament; his forehead finely proportioned; his eyes light-coloured, brilliant, acute, and deeply penetrating; his nose rather aquiline; his mouth betokened delicacy of feeling, his whole countenance expressed liability to irritation, great sensibility, clear understanding, and exalted virtue."

Two months after his return from his last visit to Ackworth he was again seized with illness, which terminated his useful busy life in about a fortnight.

His death took place on the 26th twelfth month, 1780, at the age of sixty-eight.

Thus died the distinguished Yorkshireman, John Fothergill, who in life had so thoroughly exemplified his own saying, *that the great business of man as a member of society is to be as useful to it as possible, in whatsoever department he may be stationed.*

Hitchin.   JAMES HACK TUKE.

---

* "The Yorkshireman," by Luke Howard.
† David Barclay was the grandson of Robert Barclay, of Ury, the distinguished author of Barclay's "Apology."

REV JAMES HILDYARD

THE Rev. James Hildyard, Rector of Ingoldsby, in Lincolnshire, and author of the Ingoldsby Letters on the Revision of the Book of Common Prayer, was born at Winestead, in Holderness, Yorkshire, on the 11th of April, 1809. He was the eighth of a family of ten sons, nine of whom were sent in due course to the University of Cambridge, where they all took their M.A. degree; six of them becoming fellows of their respective colleges. The most conspicuous of these youths was Robert Charles, the third son in point of seniority, who for many years represented Whitehaven in Parliament, and who was well-known among his contemporaries as an ardent Tory of the old school.

James, the subject of our present memoir, was a very delicate boy from his early infancy, and was in consequence put out to nurse; to which circumstance he probably owes the preservation of his life. At the age of eleven he was placed under the charge of the celebrated Dr. Butler, Master of Shrewsbury, at which school the present Archbishop of York, and the Bishops of Manchester and St. Davids' were also educated, though all of them of junior standing to the Rector of Ingoldsby.

He became head of the school, which then numbered upwards of three hundred scholars, at the age of seventeen, and remained head boy for three years, being detained a year longer than the usual period of leaving school owing to the delicacy of his constitution. His immediate contemporaries, at that time, were the late Dean of Wells (Johnson), and present Dean of Rochester (Scott), the Principal of Brazennose College, Oxford (Cradock) and the late Master of St. John's College, Cambridge (Bateson).

He showed a singular spirit of independence, even in those early days, as heading a Rebellion known to this day among the Salopians, though happening more than fifty years ago, as the "Beef Row;" arising from a not ill-founded resistance to the scanty, if not unwholesome diet then supplied to the boys, but which, we believe, has been since considerably improved, probably owing to the spirited outbreak exhibited under our hero in April, 1829.

In the October term of that year, he entered as a Pensioner at Christ's College, Cambridge, of which the then head was the late Dr. Kaye Bishop of Lincoln. It was mainly owing to the bishop's influence that our promising undergraduate was at once elected to a Tancred Divinity Studentship, worth, at that time, about £111 per annum, and tenable up to the degree of Master of Arts. This was a great relief to the purse of his father, who had made every sacrifice to send all his children to college, with the exception of one, the fourth son, who, of his own free choice, elected to pursue the mercantile profession. In the course of his undergraduate career, Mr. Hildyard was pre-eminently successful; ranking in this respect on a par with the Wordsworths and Kennedys, whose names it is sufficient to mention

Believe me

Yrs faithfully

Ingoldsby

in order to determine the scale of academical distinction to which Mr. Hildyard belongs.

In January, 1833, he graduated as a senior Optime in Mathematics, Second in the First Class of the Classical Tripos, and Chancellor's Medallist, and was immediately thereupon elected Fellow of his College, where, in due course, he became Classical Lecturer and Tutor, till finally he accepted the retired living of Ingoldsby, in the gift of the College, upon which he married, and where he has resided without intermission for the last seven and thirty years.

We must not, however, pass over too rapidly the record of Mr. Hildyard's residence (which lasted for fourteen years), as an energetic member of the governing body in the University. Those of his contemporaries who survive will bear testimony to his indomitable zeal and activity in promoting a variety of college and academical reforms.

He greatly improved the method of individual college tuition, waging war to the knife with the then much-abused practice of private tuition, upon which subject he wrote more than one pamphlet, exposing it as a system of *cram*, which we fear it *still is* to a great extent, rather than of sound and fundamental instruction. He also advocated both from the pulpit of St. Mary's, and in the local newspaper, and again through the medium of pamphlets, what was at that time called " The Voluntary Theological Examination "—that is to say, an examination not compulsory, but voluntarily accepted, after their B.A. degree, by candidates for Holy Orders. This scheme was much patronised in those days by several of the bishops, and if it has since failed to produce the fruit it was intended and calculated to do, the failure is largely due to the examination having been made too hard and repulsive for the ordinary class of theological students, and so deterring them from willingly facing an ordeal where they incurred the danger of discredit by rejection, while no immediate or appreciable advantage was to he gained by success.

Mr. Hildyard about this time was busily engaged in publishing a laborious and learned edition of some of the plays of Plautus, with Latin notes and glossary ; an edition, which, we believe, is acknowledged by all who have read the plays, to be invaluable to the student of that obscure author, while it placed the editor at the very top of the tree of Latin Scholarship amongst his contemporaries, whether at home or abroad.

At this period, also, Mr. Hildyard occupied for two years the post of Cambridge Preacher at the Chapel Royal, Whitehall, to which he was appointed by the late Bishop Blomfield. A selection from the sermons he then delivered was afterwards published by Messrs. Rivingtons, and (for a marvel in sermon publication) was rapidly sold, the Chapel having been crowded to overflowing during the months (in the season) for which he was the preacher. It was on this occasion he fought successfully the battle of the Black Gown *versus* the Surplice in the pulpit, with his Oxford colleague—the Rev. Mr. Oakley, who shortly afterwards went over to Rome—and won it; the bishop, himself, after a private interview with both preachers, giving the decision on Mr. Hildyard's side.

He was also Senior Proctor during the last year of his residence in the University; which being the year of Prince Albert's election to the Chancellorship, brought him a good deal to the front as a principal official at the ceremonies on that occasion.

During four different Long Vacations at this period of his life, Mr. Hildyard made extensive tours on the Continent, a matter not so easily accomplished in those days, when scarcely a single mile of his travels could be performed by rail. He thus visited almost the whole of Germany, Holland, Austria, Switzerland, France, Italy, Sicily, extending his tour even to Greece, Smyrna, and Constantinople, in all of which places he spent more or less time, profitably as well as pleasurably, making notes of his travels, and thus (after the fashion of old Ulysses) acquiring wisdom by the simple process of observing the manners and customs, as well as the cities, of many men. The readers of Morley's Life of Cobden will notice how exactly Mr. Hildyard's career at this epoch corresponds to that of the great Corn Law Repealer. At Athens Mr. Hildyard was laid up with the Greek fever, and narrowly escaped with his life, having been bled profusely (as was the almost universal practice in those days) by King Otho's German physician, who promised to call again and take more blood from him the following morning.

Our subject's energy of character here stood him in good service, and rescued him from this imminent catastrophe; for feeling refreshed by the early breeze about three o'clock in the morning—it being the month of June—he insisted, in spite of considerable opposition from his attendants, on being taken town to the Piræus, where the steamer was appointed to sail for Nauplia at six; and being placed on the open deck, was so carried across the splendid Ægean to Argos, and within twenty-four hours was able to inspect the Tomb of Agamemnon and the Walls of Heraclea, two of the most remarkable sights in that little known and less visited part of the Peninsula. After this, returning to Athens, he sailed for Smyrna and Constantinople—from which latter place he again took the steamer up the Danube for Vienna, to avoid the quarantine of three weeks to which he would have been subjected had he returned home as originally intended, by way of Odessa, Moscow, and St. Petersburg.

In consequence of this alteration in his plans, he had again the misfortune to be severely handled by the Danube ague, from which, however, he was once more delivered, and finding himself at last safely deposited in England, he made an inward resolution, from which he has not since departed, that no temptation whatever should seduce him to quit its peaceful and happy shores again, having come to the conclusion, after all his wanderings and wide experience, that it is, upon

INGOLDSBY RECTORY.
(South View).

INGOLDSBY RECTORY.
(North View.)

the whole, the most favoured country out of the many it has been his fortune to visit.

Shortly after this Mr. Hildyard accepted the retired living of Ingoldsby, in the southern and best part of the county of Lincoln, and upon this he vacated his Scholarship at Christ's College, and married the only daughter of George Kinderley, Esq., of Lincoln's Inn, by whom he has had two daughters, now living, and one son, who died in early infancy.

Words can hardly describe the wretched condition in which he found the parish, both morally and physically, upon his coming into possession of the living in June, 1846. His predecessor had died insolvent at the age of 84, occupying an old-tumble-down residence, scarcely distinguishable from a common barn, with not a fence, road, or even a shrub or flower of any description to meet the eye. The church was, if possible, in even a more disgraceful state ; and the parish, as may well be supposed, utterly demoralised. Mr. Hildyard's normal energy of character, however, did not forsake him even here, and in the course of two or three years he produced what might well be described as a complete " tranformation scene," where all was before absolute desolation, in fact it may be truly said of this parish under its present Rector, as of Rome under Augustus, " *Lateritiam invenit ; marmorlam reliquit.*"

And here we cannot help making a remark upon the law of dilapidations, as at present administered in the Church. In place of the old ruined rectory, for which (owing to the insolvency of his predecessor) he received only ten shillings in the pound dilapidations, Mr. Hildyard has erected, at a cost of nearly £3,000, an admirable and most substantial residence, for which his successor will have nothing to pay ; and yet, upon application, Mr. Hildyard is assured by " the authorities " in these matters, that his representatives will be liable for dilapidations, not only on this most commodious residence, built entirely by himself, but also on the remaining wreck of the old rectory, which, at the cost of about £50, he has converted into a coach-house, laundry, etc., nothing of the kind existing on the premises when he came into possession. Mr. Hildyard is told that he has no redress. If reform is anywhere needed in the Church, it is imperatively demanded here.

Surely the clergy are as much entitled, (or should be), to compensation for unexhausted improvements as tenant farmers.

Mr. Hildyard has for nearly a quarter of a century promoted, by every means and appliance within his power, a new and thorough Revision of the Book of Common Prayer. His opinions on this subject are fully and lucidly set forth in two handsome 8vo. volumes, of 800 pages, now circulating in their fourth edition.*

---

* "The Ingoldsby Letters (1858-1878) in reply to the Bishops in Convocation, the House of Lords, and elsewhere, on the Revision of the Book of Common Prayer, by the Rev. James Hildyard, B. D. Cassell, Petter & Galpin, 1879."

As these letters are unique of their kind, and have undoubtedly contributed largely to call public attention to the matter of which they treat, it may be as well to say something about them. They have been compared by one of their reviewers to the "Lettres Provinciales" of Pascal, by another to Peter Plymley's Letters by the inimitable Sydney Smith; others have compared our author to Cobbett, Bright, and Cobden, for the marvellous perseverance with which he has pursued his object in the teeth of enormous class interests and antiquated prejudices. The next generation will probably witness the entire adoption of Mr. Hildyard's views, as the present is already largely profiting by a partial recognition of them, as is pointed out in several instances in the notes to the fourth and latest edition of the letters. Should a fifth edition (as is not improbable) be called for, the work will become a complete Church History of the exciting period of the last twenty-five years, perhaps upon the whole the most remarkable of any since the Reformation under Edward VI., and Elizabeth.

Mr. Hildyard's leisure moments from this chief occupation (which has involved, as may well be believed, an enormous amount of correspondence, and other manual labour), have been spent in writing some short moral reflections, after the manner of the great Boyle, which have appeared from time to time in the Parish Magazine and Fireside. As a preacher, his style is something after that of Spurgeon, extempore, rapid, earnest, and replete with anecdote and images from every-day life, diversified largely with Scripture references, of which he is a complete master.

His health has unfortunately suffered slightly from a severe operation which he underwent some thirteen years ago, the effects of which have been to make him prefer a quiet sedentary life to the more active positions in his profession. But for this cause we are persuaded we should not at this moment be speaking of the Rev. James Hildyard as the Rector of an obscure country parish, though probably if he were to be even at this eleventh hour offered higher preferment, his answer would be in all sincerity " Nolo Episcopari," (especially in the present distracted state of the Church) : "Permit me to die, as I have lived the best part of my life, among my own people,"

"The world forgetting, by the world forgot."

He will not, however, be so easily forgotten; and it will in all likelihood be long said of the author of " The Ingoldsby Letters " when he is gone, " He being dead, yet speaketh."[*]

From THE BIOGRAPH.

---

[*] For other interesting particulars of the Hildyard family of Winestead, in Holderness, see article "The Hildyards of Winestead" under the heading of "Ancient Families" in the present volume, and for the "Arms of Hildyard" see page 1. A more extended notice of this ancient and honourable family is to be met with in Poulson's *History of Holderness.*—ED.

JOHN SYKES

THOUGH not born in the county, the subject of our sketch has been so long and honourably connected with it, both as a physician and zealous antiquary, that we have pleasure in presenting the readers of " Old Yorkshire" with his portrait and a brief notice of his life. Many of those persons whose tastes have led them into writing on antiquarian matters have been indebted to him for valuable information on genealogical and kindred subjects.

John Sykes, M.D., son of the Rev. George Sykes, was born at Paisley, Renfrewshire, 16th July, 1816. From early youth he developed a taste for antiquarian pursuits, and having studied medicine, he established himself as a physician in Doncaster, where he has been long known as able in his profession and zealous in the cultivation of his literary and antiquarian tastes. During his career he has ever been ready to assist with his valuable knowledge on genealogical subjects any student in that branch of antiquities, and this has led to a valuable and pleasant correspondence with antiquaries in all parts of the country. Though most ardently devoted to the department of antiquarian knowledge, embracing genealogy and the compilation of pedigrees, he has always taken a deep interest in whatever relates to the antiquities of Yorkshire. Dr. Sykes possesses the genealogical MSS. of the late Mr. T. N. Ince, of Wakefield, who is remembered as a diligent and painstaking collector of Yorkshire and Derbyshire pedigrees. He has also in his possession a considerable number of letters from the late Mr. Joseph Hunter, relating to Wakefield and Doncaster families. Dr. Sykes is a member of several antiquarian societies, is on the council of the Yorkshire Archæological and Topographical Society, and in 1868 had the gratification of being elected a Fellow of the Society of Antiquaries. In 1876 he was placed on the Commission of the Peace for the Borough of Doncaster.

Morley, near Leeds.   THE EDITOR,

RALPH THORESBY

AN eminent antiquarian and topographer, was born at the house of his father, John Thoresby, in Kirkgate, Leeds, August 16th, 1658. The family was ancient and respectable, and our antiquary was willing to accept the evidence of genealogists by profession, that it might be traced to Aykfith or Aykfrith, a noble baron, lord of Dent, Sedberg, and twelve other seigniories in the time of Canute, the Dane. From that period they are found in the situation of the lords of the manor of Thursby, Thorsby, Thoresby, or, as the name of the place is now pronounced, Thuresby, in Wensleydale. The direct male line continued to Henry Thoresby, a lawyer of eminence, who died in 1615, leaving a single daughter and heiress, Eleanor, who, by marriage with Sir T.

Thoresby's House, Kirkgate, Leeds.

Hardresse, of Great Hardresse, in Kent, brought the manor of Thoresby, with a large personal fortune, into that family. Henry had a younger brother, Ralph Thoresby, settled, in what capacity we are not told, at Woolham, near Barnard Castle. Ralph was the father of George Thoresby, of West Cottingwith, in the county of York, who by two successive marriages had issue John and Paul. These brothers of the half blood settled as clothiers at Leeds, where both became aldermen of the borough. The elder had a son of his own name, our author's father, and the younger had a very numerous issue. The father, a merchant, was possessed of a good share of learning, and had a particular turn to the knowledge of antiquities, which disposition was inherited by his son. Ralph Thoresby, the subject of this memoir, received the first rudiments of learning in the school, formerly the chantry, near the bridge at Leeds. He was next removed to the Grammar School, and afterwards placed by his father's care with a worthy relative in London, in order to acquire the knowledge of his intended calling as a merchant. Here, however, a new and splendid scene of antiquities opened upon him, and he seems to have been more occupied in visiting churches and other remarkable places, copying monumental inscriptions, and drawing up tables of benefactions, than in poring over ledgers, drawing up invoices, or copying the unamusing articles of a merchant's desk. In the spring of 1678, being now in his twentieth year, he was sent by his father to Rotterdam, in order to learn the Dutch and French languages, and to perfect himself in mercantile accomplishments. The climate not agreeing with his constitution, he returned to England about the close of the same year with the remains of an ague, which nothing but air and exercise could dissipate. For this purpose he made several excursions on horseback, constantly uniting the purpose of recruiting his health with the desire of topographical knowledge. By the death of his father, in 1679, the mercantile concerns of the house devolved upon the son at no very auspicious period. The woollen manufacture—the old and staple trade of the town had for a season fallen into a state of decay. To repair this deficiency, Ralph Thoresby purchased the freedom of an incorporated company of merchant adventurers trading to Hamburg, and having placed his affairs, as he supposed, in a promising situation, he married at Ledsham, near Leeds, Feb. 25, 1684, Anna, third daughter and co-heiress of Richard Sykes, of Leeds, gentleman, whose descent he has carefully recorded. But though merchandise was his profession, yet learning and antiquities were his great delight; and they took so firm a possession of his heart, that, contenting himself with a moderate patrimony, he made them the great employment of his life. His father had left him a valuable collection of coins and medals, purchased from the executors of Sir Thomas, Lord Fairfax (1611-1671), to whom and to whose family the Thoresbys had, from similarity of principles, religious and political, been long devoted. Like the old general of the Parliament, they were moderate Presbyterians, but without any violent animosity to the Church; like him they were never undevoted to the person of King Charles I., and with him they made an unqualified

Drawing Room, Thoresby's House.

76

submission to his son. After the accession of King James, and when his conduct, however plausible towards the Dissenters, threatened the ruin of Protestantism in all its denominations, he became more frequent in his attendance upon the worship of the Established Church. For this he had two reasons—first, the learned and excellent discourses of his parish minister, the Rev. John Milner, B.D.; and, secondly, a generous resolution to support by his countenance and example that Church, to the existence of which it was supposed that the Dissenters would finally be indebted for their own. Mr. Thoresby was well respected by those of the clergy and gentry, in his town and neighbourhood, who had any taste for learning or regard for piety; and he was not more diligent to increase his learned treasure, than ready to communicate it to others. It would be, in a manner, endless to enumerate the assistances which he gave in one way or another to the works of the learned. The new edition of Camden's *Britannia*, in 1695, introduced our author to Dr. Gibson, at whose request he wrote notes and additional observations on the West-Riding of Yorkshire; and for the use of this edition he transmitted above a hundred of his coins to Mr. Obadiah Walker, who had undertaken that province which related to the Roman, British, and Saxon moneys. And when the bishop was preparing that work for another and more complete impression, he sent a great number of queries to Mr. Thoresby; which were answered entirely to his lordship's satisfaction, and accompanied with other miscellaneous observations. Mr. Thomas Hearne requested Mr. Thoresby's correspondence, and often acknowledged the favour of it in print. Mr. Strype was obliged to him for communicating some original letters in his collection. His skill in heraldry and genealogy rendered him, moreover, a very serviceable correspondent to Mr. Arthur Collins in his *Peerage of England*, and made him an acceptable acquaintance to the principal persons of the College of Arms, at London. By these good offices, and by that easiness of access which he allowed to his own cabinet, he always found the like easy access to the cabinets of other virtuosoes, which gave him frequent opportunities of enlarging his collection far beyond what could have been expected from a private person not wealthy. His collection was in such esteem that not only many of the nobility and gentry of our own country, but likewise many foreigners, visited his museum, and honoured his *Album* with their names and mottoes. Among other virtuosoes, Mr. Thoresby commenced an early friendship with the celebrated naturalist, Dr. Martin Lister. It was to him that he sent an account of some Roman antiquities he had discovered in Yorkshire, which, being communicated by Dr. Lister, and Dr. Gale, Dean of York, to the Royal Society, obtained him a fellowship of that learned body, into which he was unanimously chosen at their anniversary meeting in 1697; and the great number of his papers which appear in their *Transactions*, relating chiefly to Roman and Saxon monuments of antiquity in the north of England, with notes upon them, and the inscription of coins, &c., show

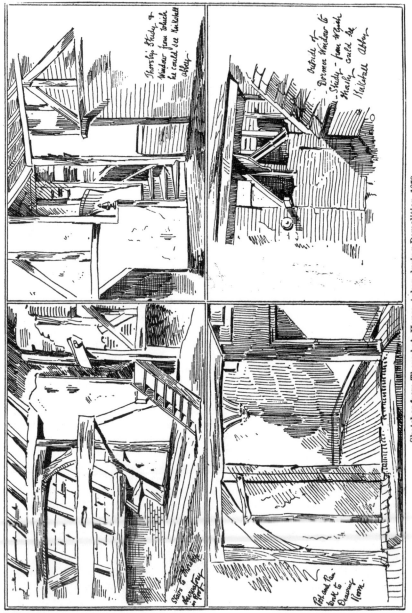

Sketches from Thoresby's House, taken during Demolition, 1878.

78

how well he deserved that honour. At what time he formed the plan of his great work the *Ducatus Leodiensis*, does not appear; but the first impulse appears to have been given by a sermon of the learned Mr. Milner, in which he took occasion to mention the great antiquity of the town, and the notice with which it had been honoured by the venerable Bede. "There is, however," says Dr. Whitaker, "a MS. belonging to the Grammar School, and, by the kindness of the late respectable master, Mr. Whiteley, now before me, containing the first rough draft of the *Ducatus*, in Thoresby's handwriting; but it has nothing to fix the date." In the prosecution of this laborious work, he frequently announces his intention of compiling an historical or *bio-graphical* part, as an accompaniment to the topographical. For this undertaking, his own museum, as well as his recollection, afforded ample materials; but age was now creeping upon him, and indolence, its usual attendant.* A regard, however, to the church of his own parish, and the many eminent divines who had presided over it, prompted him to compose and commit to the press his *Vicaria Leodiensis; or, The History of the Church of Leeds*, &c. (8vo.), which was published in 1724. He was now sixty-six years of age—a period beyond which little space is usually left for bodily or mental exertion. He had a constitutional, perhaps an hereditary, tendency to apoplexy. The consistency of his blood was thick, which exposed him to pains or numbness in the back part of his head, with other apoplectic symptoms. All these he received as intimations of his approaching departure which was delayed beyond his expectation. In the month of October, 1724, he was suddenly seized by a paralytic stroke, from which he so far recovered as to speak intelligibly and walk without help. There is also a letter extant, written by him in this melancholy state, and complaining, though with great patience and submission, of his feelings; thus he languished till the same month of the following year, when he received a second and final shock from the same disease, which put an end to his life, October 16th, 1725, in the sixty-eighth year of his age. He was interred with his ancestors in the choir of the Leeds parish church, and lay for upwards of a century without any memorial from the piety of his friends, or the gratitude of his townsmen. A memorial stone within the altar-rail at the south-east side of the parish church now bears this inscription:—"Sacred to the memory of Ralph Thoresby, F.R.S., a member of the ancient Corporation of Leeds. He was born 16th August, 1658. He died 16th October, 1725, and was interred within these walls. His character for learning is best seen in the books he published, which show him to have been a great master of the

---

* In this work he had proceeded so far as to bring his narration, in a fair copy, nearly to the end of the sixth century, illustrating and confirming his history by his coins, &c. This curious piece being found well prepared for the press, as far as it extends, and well worthy of the public acceptance, is inserted in the *Biographia Britannica*, in order to excite some able hand to carry it on, and complete the noble design of the author.

history and antiquities of his own county; to attain which it became necessary for him to be thoroughly skilled, as he was, in genealogy and heraldry. He appears from these books to have been also an industrious biographer. That, however, which set his reputation the highest as a scholar, was his uncommon knowledge of both coins and medals. Thoresby was intimate with some of the most excellent and estimable men of his day; among them were Dr. Sharpe, Archbishop of York; Dr. Nicholson, afterwards Bishop of Carlisle; Dr. Gibson, afterwards Bishop of London; Dr. Gale, Dean of York; Dr. George Hickes, Bishop Kennet, Thomas Hearne, John Strype, John Ray, Dr. Richardson, of Bierley; Sir Hans Sloane, John Evelyn, Dr. Mead, and Dr. Stukeley. He was a man beloved as well as esteemed and valued for the warmth of his affections, and the endowments of his mind.

The works of this fine old antiquary comprise :—The "Ducatus Leodiensis; or the Topography of Leeds and Parts Adjacent." London, 1715 ; folio. It is dedicated to the Marquis of Carmarthen, and contains a list of subscribers occupying six pages. "Vicaria Leodiensis ; or the History of the Church in Leeds, Yorkshire." London, 1724 ; 8vo. Is dedicated to Archbishop Dawes. "Ralph Thoresby's Diary" (1674-1724), now first published from the original manuscripts by the Rev. Joseph Hunter. "Letters of Eminent Men addressed to him," now first published from the originals. London, 1832 ; 8vo. Two volumes.

Swaledale. R. V. TAYLOR, B.A.

SIR MARTIN FROBISHER

OME members of the Frobisher family moved from Chirk, in North Wales, to Yorkshire, about the middle of the fourteenth century; the orthography of their patronymic being Furbisher, Furbiser, or Ffourbyssher. In both localities they allied themselves with old county families. The art of marrying well was one of their accomplishments. In Yorkshire the family centred around Altofts, in the parish of Normanton. One John Frobisher, of that place, was farmer of the king's demesne, and married to the daughter of Sir W. Scargell. His grandson, Francis, was Mayor and Recorder of Doncaster. The brother of Francis was named Bernard who married the daughter of a knight named York. To them were born John, Davy, Jane, Martin, and Margaret. The last-named was baptised in Normanton on February 10, 1541. Bernard Frobisher was buried at the same place on September 1, 1542.

From these considerations there can be little doubt that Martin was born between 1530-40, at Altofts. The mother, to relieve herself of a share of the burden of bringing up five children, sent Martin to her brother, Sir John York, then residing in London. An additional reason for this transfer of the boy was that there were no suitable schools in his native place.

Sir John observed that his nephew was a youth 'of great spirit and bold courage and natural hardness of body,' which, in our phraseology, would run—brave, high-mettled, and with a good constitution. Whether his maternal uncle disliked the charge which he had undertaken, or found the 'great spirit' more than he could guide, or that young Martin would rove like any adventurous boy, matters little now, for to sea he went soon after his arrival in London.*

There happened to be a small fleet of merchant ships on the point of sailing for the Coast of Guinea. The admiral was John Lock, and this was in the year 1554. Martin was placed on board one of these ships, and sailed away upon what was then deemed a very long voyage and to but half-discovered places. The fleet returned in the following year, having been very prosperous. This was the first effort of the English to establish a permanent trade in African gold and ivory. The youth's first voyage confirmed him in the choice of a calling. To the end of his days he continued a sailor.

When Frobisher first emerged out of the seclusion of home and Yorkshire, a lad ' of great spirit and bold courage and natural hardness of body,' he came not, as a young Hannibal or Drake, with a paternal vengeance to be wreaked on the enemy of his nation and religion. He was just such an ardent, adventure-loving boy as one may find in a mess of middies on board any of our own Queen's ships.

With superabundant faith in the heroic, and happily endowed with the strength and courage necessary for bringing forth the works of that faith, he was flung of by his maternal uncle and fell on his feet in that paradise of boys, the forecastle of a rover, and perhaps a slaver.

He possessed only the education which a mother gives to her youngest boy; he could read, and almost write a large round hand. But he was overflowing with latent greatness. He took with him a fortune which can be estimated in no symbols arithmetical or algebraic —the inheritance of noble qualities descended from an ancestry of gentlemen bound to honour and duty more than life.

In such a school, where right must always ally itself with might, where authority is only to be preserved with a hard word, and sometimes a harder blow, the noble qualities developed. It was the case of an oak planted on a seaward cliff, whose branches are toughened by

---

* A writer in "Notes and Queries" says that "The biographical accounts of Sir Martin Frobisher state that his parents were in very humble circumstances, and the date of his birth as unknown. Dr. Miller, however, in his *History and Antiquities of Doncaster*, p. 117, says, that "Francis Frobisher was Mayor of Doncaster in the year 1535, and from his supposed age, compared with that of Sir Martin's, was most probably the father of this naval hero. Unfortunately the parish register does not commence the baptisms till the year 1558, and Sir Martin must have been born long before that period. However, I have found the baptisms of several of his relations, viz., 1561, May 30, Christian, daughter of William Frobisher. 1564, Mar. 2, Darcye, son of William Frobisher. 1566, Mar. 18, Matthew, son of the same. 1567, Jan. 18, Elizabeth, daughter of the same.' Dr. Miller then adds in a note the following extract from Maneser's *Account of Yorkshire Families*—' The father of Sir Martin Frobisher resided at Finningley, his mother was daughter to Mr. Rogers, of Everton, his grandfather William married Margaret, daughter of Wm. Boynton, of Barmston, Esq. His great-grandfather Francis was Recorder of Doncaster, and married Christian, daughter of Sir Brian Hastings, Knt., and purchased lands at Doncaster.' "

the boisterous gales, and are at the same time stunted and deformed.

The rough life of the privateering captain, with its ready expediences in the face of unexpected perils, its many temptations to plunge into piracy, its sufferings from hunger and thirst, its quelling of mutinies with a keen, broad partizan—all this is lost for us. Yet one needs no predominance of imagination to picture Frobisher's ten years of roving. He was a youthful commander. A voyage out of the sight of land was almost a novelty; the rocks, shoals, and currents of the ocean were marked on no chart; the degrees of longitude were put down of the same width from pole to pole; no law was acknowledged on the high seas; pirates infested even the mouth of the Thames; and yet in a Liliputian bark the English mariner was prepared to roam over unknown seas.

Either his meeting with Michael Lock or Humphrey Gilbert touched a secret spring in the young captain's soul which opened a chamber hitherto dark and uninhabited. Lock had long been drawn ' to the study of cosmography,' and had convinced himself of the existence of a North-West Passage to Cathay. Humphrey Gilbert had arrived at the same conclusion, and published a pamphlet to prove it, in which he mingles Homer and mathematics, deducting a second Magellan's Straits from the *primum mobile,* and quoting Esther and Ahasuerus to show that there was a good market for calicoes in the far East.

The interest awakened by the speculations of these theorists doubtless saved Frobisher from sinking into lawlessness. He was on the point of becoming a confirmed buccaneer. Henceforth he had a noble object which lifted him above the low level into which he had drifted, and privateering became a means to an end, as the primary school to the youthful village master who spends his evenings reading for a profession. After his return from each voyage he hastened to Lock's house to listen to the conjectures of the retired master mariner, pore over his charts of imaginary coasts and channels, and gather from Doctor Dee all that the great astrologer and cosmographer was pleased to communicate. To pursue for fifteen years the noble purpose of sailing a ship ' by the West to the East ' was in itself something, though the quest had never been made. His unmeasured courage and perseverance were exhibited in the voyage and dangers of the ' Gabriel.' His readiness of resource came out on every occasion of dismaying peril. His great physical strength completed his endowment for the work before him. His skill in seamanship was tried in making three successful entrances into Frobisher's Straits, which to this day are a region avoided by every mariner. He was the first man who ever went in search of the North-West Passage; and he was the first Englishman who ever attempted to establish a colony on the American continent, although the spirit of discovery within him was by the force of circumstances subordinated to the venturers' greed for gold. He took the first Protestant missionary to the New World, and by him the Sacrament of the Lord's Supper was for the first time administered according to Protestant rites on that continent.

Fuller says of his character—'He was very valiant, but withal harsh and violent (faults which may be dispensed with in one of his profession).' This has been repeated by almost every subsequent writer who has made any sketch of the Admiral's life. Campbell's paraphrase of this charge is—'A true patriot, yet in his carriage blunt, and a very strict observer of discipline, even to a degree of severity, which hindered his being beloved.' If Campbell supposed any of Queen Elizabeth's great captains was 'perfumed like a milliner, holding a pouncet box 'twixt his finger and his thumb,' he is not wrong in applying to Frobisher the word blunt. It is a quality not more rare in a sailor than courtliness in a groom of the chamber. But Campbell is not justified in making Fuller's words mean that Frobisher was a martinet and unbeloved. The only circumstance that could be wrung to support such an assertion is a phrase in a letter of Raleigh's to Sir Robert Cecil when the command of the expedition of 1592 was transferred from himself to Frobisher. 'I have promised Her Majesty,' writes Raleigh, 'that *if I can persuade the Companies to follow Sir Martin Frobisher* I will without fail return.' The hypothesis means no more than that the expedition being composed of and equipped by the personal friends of Raleigh, they would naturally be unwilling to trust their lives and fortunes to any other commander, though he should be the most skilful in the world. There are many reasons for holding the contrary opinion of the knight's character. One of Master Sellman's accusations was that Frobisher was so lax in his discipline and lenient to the petty officers and mariners that no order could be kept on board. Again, no voyager of his time had so few mutinies. The 'Michael' and 'Thomas' of Ipswich alone deserted him. But the officers of both those vessels thought their Admiral drowned before they turned cravens. The experience of Drake with the ready execution block, and of gentle John Davis was to have their subalterns mutiny in their very presence. Frobisher's oft repeated efforts to regain his five men captured by the Esquimaux, and the sacrifices he was prepared to make to accomplish that purpose, exibit the humane side of his character. In his letter after the capture of Fort Crozon he says, when referring to Norris's request for some of his men—'The mariners are very unwilling to go except I go with them myself, yet if I find it come to an extremity we will try what we are able.'

Fuller's meaning is, doubtless, that Frobisher was possessed of a violent temper. But the passionate men are not usually the unbeloved. The severe martinet is more often the dapper, cultured, cool, low-speaking officer, than the rude, herculean, boisterous sailor. Frobisher had never learned how to put a bridle on his indignation. Any suspicion of sham or wrong put him instantly ablaze, the consequence being that he raised against himself a host of needless enemies.

He was a man heartily loved and heartily hated. And as for the coarse epithets which he employed in his moments of anger, his Queen was painted with the same brush; while for the Admiral there is the excuse that with all men the ugly phrases, half-forgotten, which still

Sir Martin Frobisher.

linger in the memory as the fruit of association with base companions, find free utterance from the choleric tongue. He was 'full of strange oaths . , . , jealous in honour, sudden and quick in quarrel.'

Although Frobisher was not tainted with the love of money he allowed himself to be led by circumstances to the commission of that which his sense of honour must have condemned, in order to procure the means for the prosecution of his great purpose. The story of Palissy pursuing his heroic quest of the glaze, deaf to a hungering family crying to him for bread, had only been told ten years before. Martin Frobisher's search for the North-West Passage, with the widow Riggatt and her numerous brood hungering at Hampstead, was a repetition of it. Of such conduct it is hard to form a just opinion, inasmuch as the judgment and the sympathies do not coincide.

He was not a man devoid of domestic virtues. He had a strong love of his kindred and a kindly affection for his faithful servants, as we learn from the provisions of his will.

But the "signal service in eighty-eight" is the chapter in his history which will always gain for him the readiest admiration. His share in the defeat of the Armada has been almost entirely attributed to Drake. Nowhere else have his achievements been so completely overshadowed. The Spaniards knew of only one English admiral, whose name was Drake, and so every desperate charge made upon the Armada was attributed to him. But no English authority has any achievement of his to record from the taking of Don Pedro's ship to the battle of Gravelines; while the Queen was so pleased with Frobisher during that crisis to the realm, that she employed no other admiral during his lifetime after the year 1589.

He had the prudence of Hawkins with the resolution and quickness of Drake, while his dauntless courage was all his own. It was valour spiced with what can only be called devilry, acquired in his privateering days. His seamanship has perhaps never been surpassed.

Elizabeth's Admirals were all great men. They had great faults as well as great virtues. It was fertile soil that produced gigantic weeds as well as heavy ears of corn. They trod the rough, thorny path of heroes. They knew not where their bodies would lie; their roving, perilous life made that uncertain. It was in God's keeping. But for their souls they were certain. Their faith in their religion and in an overruling Providence—who helped them in storms and among icebergs, who wrought for them continual miracles of deliverance, who confounded the knavish designs of their foes, and always protected their Queen, giving her the victory over all her enemies—would raise a laugh of scorn in the barracks or forecastle of our day. They had an adoring loyalty, an unwavering faith in the unseen, both good and evil, very rare now. Satan is not terrible to men who have refined him out of their creed; but those old worthies believed in the Devil, and yet feared him no more than the Spaniard. The man who did his duty to God and his country needed not to fear anything, seen or unseen. That much they knew and lived; and in that faith they died, leaving the rest to God and their Saviour.

London. FRANK JONES, B.A

86

JOHN HOLLAND

John Holland was born March 14th 1794, and died December 28th, 1872. The house in which he was born was his happy home through life. At the beginning of this century it was conspicuous on the hill-side in Sheffield Park. The cottage still stands, but its surroundings have been greatly changed. Other buildings have been added to it; houses extend now from the town to the garden wall; and a handsome Board School has been built at the bottom of the field in which Holland played when a boy. The following lines refer to what the engraving represents :—

> " Hard by, with no distinguished features graced,
> Devoid of beauty, ornament, and taste,
> The eye of friendship views the humble spot,
> Where first the Muse endeared her votary's lot;
> Home of my youth and cradle of my joys,
> Though greatness scorn, and wealth or pride despise,
> Dearer to me this mansion of my birth,
> Than all the prouder structures of the earth :
> When travelled wonder hath told all it can,
> And wearied art exhausted all on man,
> HOME still is sweet, is still, where'er we look,
> The loveliest picture in creation's book. "

For a time he was employed with his father as an optician, but books pleased him more than telescope tubes ; and his studious habits were encouraged in various ways. Good results soon appeared. Many of the defects of his school education were supplied. He read his books and re-read them until their contents were made his own. Thus his mind was fully brought under discipline, and thus he attained great proficiency, and literary pursuits became their own ample reward. For a time he had to live by his pen, but afterwards, needing no payment, he did much literary work for which he refused pecuniary recompense, because to have accepted material remuneration would have lessened his pleasure in writing.

From early days John Holland was faithfully devoted to the Muse. He was meditative and became fond of solitude and of country walks. He made books his companions, and went to them with a pure affection

---

* *Old Yorkshire*, vol. 3, p. 50.

† *The Life of John Holland, of Sheffield Park*, from numerous Letters and other Documents furnished by his Nephew and Executor, John Holland Brammall. With Portrait and Illustrations, by the Rev. William Hudson. London : Longmans, Green, & Co., 1874.

John Holland.

when the less agreeable tasks of the day were done. And the thoughts of men and the works of God stirred his soul, and made him long to be a poet. He says :—

> "Sweet Poesy, thy numbers
>   Entranced me while a boy,
> Thrilled through my golden slumbers
>   And through my waking joy ;
> And when thy sounds ascended
>   With some immortal name,
> With them my spirit blended,
>   I sighed for hopeless fame.
>
> I lived but to discover
>   Thy beauty and thy pride :
> In youth thou wast my lover,
>   In manhood's dawn my bride :
> I loved on airy pinion,
>   Free as the birds in spring,
> Through Fancy's wide dominion,
>   With thee to soar and sing."

The life thus begun was consistent to its end. In his prime he wrote :—

> "They tell me that, not as in pride of youth
>   Love I sweet POESY ; as if the joy
>   Of ripened feeling could grow stale, or cloy,
> Or time outwear the relish of ripe truth.
> It is not so ; the tones and tales of ruth
>   Touch all life's inner harmonies, and still
>   Endear the concert between chance and will,
> Whate'er the world's harsh claims ; and I, in sooth,
> Own now, as ever, little, the strong spells
>   Of wealth, and strife, and pride, and place, and power,
>   To which tired man, through being's fretful hour,
> Yields body, spirit, soul. True, one who dwells
> With duty must yield service. With a sigh,
> I grant things change about me, but not I."

Though Mr. Holland lived and died a bachelor, yet from youth to age he was deeply impressed by womanly grace. Many of the most beautiful of his poems were addressed to ladies ; and here is a characteristic sonnet : —

> "The man who takes not from a female hand
>   The sweetest common cup of daily life,
> Or whether in the world's thick ranks he stand
>   A mighty struggler in the common strife,
>   Or, cut by Superstition's felon knife
> From Nature's genial law, in lonesome cell
> He find himself for ever doomed to dwell,
>   Uncheered by mother, sister, daughter, wife,
> May well be deemed, whate'er his sterner claim,
>   Humanity's Enigma ! Friendship, grace,
>   The past, the future of his father's race
> He lives but to reproach with silent shame,—
> Unmeet for earth, undisciplined for heaven,
> While spurning in God's name the help-meet God has given."

He was as remarkable for tenderness of feeling. A pathetic incident touched him, and he would then express his thoughts in verse ;

and his poem was generally a sonnet. This was a striking feature in Mr. Holland One example may be given here. He transcribed a poetical and touching story about a funeral which is told in Andersen's *Hartz Mountains*, and penned the following sonnet on "The Bird and the Burial," which probably had a local occasion :—

"In a small garret in yon narrow street,
    Lay a poor corpse, and near it, in despair,
    Sat a lorn widow weeping, wondering where
And how to get plain grave and winding sheet,—
When, lo ! the casement open, a bright bird,
A strayed Canary, fluttered in, and sweet
    Its note began, perched on the dead ! Glad heard
The mourner this strange omen, and, as meet,
    Deemed it a timely heaven-sent gift, and caught
    The warbler, which, to its glad owner brought,
Was ransomed with a noble piece of gold.
    Then the bereaved one, grateful for the sign,
Gave her dead husband to the hallowed mould,
Acknowledging the hand of Providence Divine."

James Montgomery.

Chief among Mr. Holland's friends was the poet James Montgomery, who encouraged him in youth and rejoiced in the achievements of his manhood, and whose biographer he eventually became. The friendship between them was very intimate, as their biographies fully show. With another townsman, Ebenezer Elliott, the celebrated "Corn Law Rhymer," for whose genius Mr. Holland had great admiration, he was much less acquainted.

JOHN HOLLAND'S BIRTH PLACE, SHEFFIELD PARK.

Another poetical friend was "Eta Mawr," the late Miss Elizabeth Colling, of Hurworth-on-Tees, who published several volumes of poems, and with whom Mr. Holland corresponded for thirty years before their first interview. This sonnet was addressed to that lady:—

"To thee, fair dweller by the Northern Tees,
　　Whose friendship—though we never met !—I've long
　　Enjoyed, through letters kind, and missive song,
　I dedicate this ryhme : with what sweet ease
　Souls, gentle, generous, and ingenious, please
　　And are pleased, 'midst life's ambitious throng
　　Of heartless, selfish aims ! Nor would I wrong
　Aught of grave, virtuous, wise, by words like these :
　Lady, whate'er of happiness, or grace,
　　Of friendship, music, books, or minstrel-art,
　Gifts of indulgent heaven ! thy dwelling place
　　Knows at this hour—ne'er may they thence depart :
　Nor fail I there, while Fancy thus can dart
　Her spell, thy presence, though unseen, to trace."

Holland's poetry is " thoughtful, pure, and elevating," and displays a cultivated mind and a well-governed fancy. " It is in almost every instance the product of a calm and happy inspiration." " In Holland passed away the last of those gifted men on whose account, during the first half of the nineteenth century, his native town was worthily designated ' classic Sheffield '.

He lived within a very short distance of the ruins of Sheffield Manor Lodge, where Mary, Queen of Scots, was long imprisoned. Those ruins, he says, were " the cradle of his earliest associations and feelings in poetry." " The winds and storms which, during his early years, accelerated the total ruination even of the ruins of ' that summer mansion of the Talbots,' rocked his feelings into ' antiquarian reverence.'" "The spice of the antiquary " which was thus early insinuated into his nature, produced manifold literary results. He loved

" The historic mirror that reveals
Scenes which our studious thoughts with quiet lessons fill."

He contributed valuable notes for a new edition of Hunter's celebrated *Hallamshire* ; he wrote early in life his *History of Worksop*, and in his old age *Wharncliffe* and *Sheffield*; and while he was the editor of a newspaper and afterwards, he was often sending forth sketches and essays in which the " spice of the antiquary " was very perceptible. He had an intimate acquaintance with the history, the antiquities, and the industries of his native district. It has been truly said that " he could always tell what nobody else could tell, and his stores of information were placed freely at the disposal of all." " Obsolete customs, superseded games, and family histories had great attractions for him, and became in his hands highly interesting themes." Many knew the value of having in the town a central referee so accessible and so worthy of reliance.

He did good work as a biographer. The " Lives " which were separately published by him fill eleven volumes, and he wrote also very many biographical sketches which appeared in various publications. *Notes and Queries, The Reliquary,* and kindred periodicals were enriched by his pen.

He composed sermons which have been read from the pulpit, and which may be still in use, wrote for various religious magazines, developed his views on matters of theological speculation, and wrote some hundreds of hymns for Sunday School anniversaries, and other occasions.

His scientific attainments were respectable. He was the author of the three volumes of Lardner's *Cabinet Cyclopædia* which treat of

The Mount, Sheffield.

Manufactures in Metal, and his *Queen of Flowers* is a literary gem which a person unable to find delight in botany could not have written. He seemed to know no unfruitful themes. To the end of his life he read extensively in many departments of knowledge; and as a man of letters he found an occupation which never ceased to give him pleasure, and which he used in order that he might "in his own generation serve the counsel of God.'

Mr. Holland was a Christian. In the Report of the Sheffield Literary and Philosophical Society, published after his death, it was said, that "his devotion to literature was only surpassed by the rare excellence of his heart and his many Christian virtues." In his daily calling, in society, and in his literary capacity he " adorned the doctrine of God our Saviour." His usual place of worship was the Wesleyan Chapel in Carver Street, where he attended the morning service with great regularity.

He died at *The Mount*, Sheffield, at the house of his nephew, within a few yards of the spot on which Montgomery had breathed his last nearly nineteen years before. A feeling which prevailed in the town when his death became known was well expressed by the Rev. John Burbidge, of St. Stephen's Church, in the following lines :—

> "Thy life was pure, holy, and good ; and when
> The great Disposer summoned thee on high,
> The lesson of that life was given ; and then,
> Calm in thy faith, thou did'st not fear to die,
> Rest in thy peace, thou hast not lived in vain ;
> Thy story, gentle bard, shall oft be told ;
> In Memory's vision shalt thou live again,
> Thy place unbought by either rank or gold,
> Lowly, but safe, among the men of old."

The following list comprises the works separately published by Mr. Holland. Some of the titles are presented in abbreviated form :—

1820.—*Sheffield Park*; a descriptive poem. Dedicated to the most noble Bernard Edward, Duke of Norfolk. Reprinted in 1859 with notes.

1820.—*The Methodist*, a poem.

1821.—*The Cottage of Pella* ; a tale of Palestine, with other poems.

1821.—*The Village of Eyam*, a poem.

1822.—*The Hopes of Matrimony* ; a poem. Second edition 1836.

1824.—*The Old Arm Chair*, or, Recollections of a Bachelor. By Sexagenarius.

1824.—*Memoirs of the Rose*; comprising botanical, poetical, and miscellaneous recollections of that celebrated flower. In a series of letters to a lady. The second edition, containing additions, improvements, and choice illustrations, and entitled *The Queen of Flowers*, was published in 1840.

1826.—*The History, Antiquitities, and Description of the Town and Parish of Worksop, in the County of Nottingham.*

1827.—*Flowers from Sheffield Park*; a selection of poetical pieces originally published in the Sheffield *Iris.* Dedicated to James Montgomery.

1827.—*Crispin Anecdotes*, comprising interesting notices of shoemakers who have been distinguished for genius, enterprise, or eccentricity; also curious particulars relative to the origin, importance, and manufacture of shoes ; with other matters illustrative of the history of the gentle craft.

1829.—*The Pleasures of Sight* ; a poem.

1830.—*Memoirs of the Life and Ministry of the Rev. John Summerfield. M.A.*, late a Preacher in connection with the Methodist Episcopal Church in America.

1830.—*Sketch of the Life and Character of the late Mr. Joseph Cowley*, Superintendent of the Red-hill Sunday School and senior secretary of the Sunday School Union, Sheffield.

1831.—*Memoir and Select Remains of Mr. George Atkinson, late of Sheffield, Surgeon.*

1831.—*A Treatise on the Progressive Improvement and Present State of the Manufactures in Metal.* 3 vols. Dr. Lardner's *Cabinet Cyclopædia.*

1832.—*Tyne Banks ; a poetical sketch by a visitor to Newcastle.*

1835.—*Cruciana ; Illustrations of the most striking aspects under which the Cross of Christ and symbols derived from it have been contemplated by piety, superstition, imagination, and taste.*

1837.—*The Tour of the Don*; a series of sketches made during a pedestrian ramble along the banks of that river and its principal tributaries. Originally published in the *Sheffield Mercury* during the year 1836. Two vols.

1840.—*Brief Notices of Animal Substances used in the Sheffield Manufactures.* Originally published in the *Sheffield Mercury*.

1841.—*The History and Description of Fossil Fuel*, or, the Collieries and Coal Trade of Great Britain.

1843.—*The Psalmists of Britain.* Records, biographical and literary, of upwards of 150 authors who have rendered the whole or part of the Book of Psalms into English verse, with specimens of the different versions, and a general introduction. Two vols., octavo. This is one of the most valuable of Mr. Holland's works.

1845.—*Poets of Yorkshire*, comprising sketches of the lives and specimens of the writings of those children of song who have been natives of, or otherwise connected with, the County of York, commenced by Wm. Cartwright Newsam, and completed by John Holland for the benefit of Mr. Newsam's family.

1845.—*Handley Church; a poetical memorial.*

1851.—*Memoirs of Sir Francis Chantrey, R.A., Sculptor in Hallamshire and elsewhere.*

1851.—*A Memoir of the History and Cultivation of the Gooseberry.*

1851.—*The Great Exhibition; a Poetical Rhapsody.*

1851.—*Diurnal Sonnets*: Three hundred and sixty-six Poetical Meditations on various subjects, Personal, Abstract, and Local.

1851.—*A Poet's Gratulation in Rhyme.* (Presented to Montgomery on his Eightieth birthday.)

1854-6.—*Memoirs of the Life and Writings of James Montgomery.* 7 vols. (The Rev. James Everett's name appears with Mr. Holland's on the title page.)

1861.—*The Bazaar, or, Money and the Church.* A Rejected Offering in blank verse. By a Christian Poet.

1864.—*Wharncliffe, Wortley, and the Valley of the Don; Photographically Illustrated by Theophilus Smith.*

1865.—*Sheffield and its Neighbourhood, Photographically Illustrated by Theophilus Smith.*

1867.—*Evenings with the Poets by Moonlight*, in a Series of Letters to a Lady.

1869.—*Our Old Churchyard.*

1870.—*A Handy Book on Matters Matrimonial.* (London: Houlston and Sons.)

These books, with his sermons, hymns, magazine articles, and "acres of newspaper matter," formed a prodigious contribution to current literature, and show that much work may be crowded into a busy life.

London, April, 1884.   WILLIAM HUDSON.

BISHOP JOHN ALCOCK

O F the biographies of Bishop Alcock that have been written, all, with one exception, have fallen into errors, which originate in Abraham De la Pryme's *Euphemeris Vitæ* It seems strange that Yorkshiremen should write a life of one of their own countrymen and fall into these errors, as only a little trouble was needed to compare facts and documents which would result in accurate information. To have left an outsider to present the only correct biography is greatly to be deplored. The authorities used by the Coopers in their *Athenæ Cantabrigienses*, were accessible to all; yet although this work has been published 26 years, it has not been recognised by the biographers of Bishop Alcock; for instance, Corlass in his *Hull Authors*, and a recent life which appeared in one of the Hull papers, all follow De la Pryme's *Euphemeris Vitæ*, like sheep following their leader.

In the following biography I have gathered all information concerning John Alcock that was accessible to me, resulting in a more expanded life of the Bishop than that given by Cooper, giving that information which is valued by his countrymen, and which was not important enough to be admitted into the *Athenæ Cantabrigienses*, a work invaluable to workers in the wide field of biography, and to libraries which pretend to be useful to historians.

John Alcock, the subject of this memoir, was born at Beverley or Hull. Biographers differ, but no one vouchsafes a definite conclusion. When we remember that the Alcocks of this period were influential merchants, and lived in Hull, it seems most probable that the last named was his native place. De la Pryme's assertion that the records show him, or his parents, as living at Hull, should be further taken up, and search made among the records of Hull, which I believe have not yet been examined, and perhaps light may be thrown upon this bone of contention. The year of his birth is unknown, but by putting evidence together, we can ascertain within a few years. William, the father of John Alcock, died 1434-5, as his will, which was dated at Hull, 1434, was proved by his widow Jan. 13, 1434-5. In this will he describes himself as ' *mercator*,' of Kingston-upon-Hull, and in it he only mentions Thomas, his son, and the others '*pueros meos*.' From this it is concluded that John and his brother Robert were under age. Then, as John died in 1500, his first preferment being in 1461, and his ordination in 1449, it may safely be concluded that he was about 10 years old when his father died. It is thought that John was the youngest.

John was not the only one of the family who distinguished himself, though not as he did; his brothers were distinguished in their own town, whereas John was known to the whole of England and Scotland. Both filled the most important offices of the town, first by being made sheriff, and eventually mayor, of Hull. Thomas was Mayor of Hull during 1478, when "the plague which had alter-"nately raged more or less from 1472, destroying near 1600 per-"sons, ceased this year, but not before it had proved the death of "this worshipful magistrate and brought his dear wife and children to "their silent graves." So says Gent in his History of Hull. It is to the memory of this brother that John, when Bishop of Worcester, built a Chapel on the south side of Trinity Church, *circa* 1478-83.

Robert Alcock, the other brother, married Katharine . . . (?) and had issue, Robert and Katharine, who married (1) John Dalton, who died 1496, and afterwards . . . Henrison, but died 1545, desiring to be buried in the ' trinity churche in the quere under the throughe wher my husband, John Dalton, liethe." Of this John Dalton, the editor of Testamenta Eboracensia says that he was the founder of that branch of Daltons which settled at Hawkswell in Richmondshire.

I may here mention that De la Pryme's recollections of the family are entirely wrong, but as I have fully explained this previously,* I need not repeat it here. His book has to be used with caution, and all the information he gives must be substantiated by evidence from other quarters.

From the Testamenta Eboracensia [II. 42] we gain the information that " He was admitted to the order of sub-deacon by John, Bishop of " Philippolis, the suffragan of the Archbishop of York, on the 8th March, " 1449, in the Abbey of Thornton, Lincolnshire, of which house he may "perhaps have been an inmate, giving him a title. He became deacon "on the 29th of March, 1449, and priest on the 12th of April following." I am unable to find from what source this valuable information has been gleaned.

It is possible that he spent the whole of the time which lays between his ordination and his first preferment, at the University of

---

* Hull Quarterly, Vol. 1, p. 93.

Cambridge, but of this we know nothing except that he proceeded to the degree of LL.D., or Doctor of Laws, at Cambridge in 1466, which was after his removal to London. To take this degree he must have resided at the University a number of years, and from this I infer that he proceeded to Cambridge immediately after his ordination. In the studies at the University of Cambridge, the study of law was an exception, and not encouraged, so very few took a law degree. The prominent study was Theology, followed by Philosophy. No doubt he went through the ordinary routine of study, as he was prepared for most of his future work by his early education. In Alcock's time Cambridge University was in a flourishing state, according to the numbers of the Colleges built during that period. But the learning of her members could not compare with the beauty of the buildings. The state of the University, as described by Erasmus, about 60 years afterwards was indeed very unsatisfactory, and if the condition of the learning at Cambridge was so then, can we not imagine what it was during Alcock's residence there at a much earlier period, before that great impulse to learning by the revival of ' the new learning ' had burst forth ?

Following the completion of his education at the University, came the offer of the living at St. Margaret's, Fish Street, London, from the hands of a friend, Thomas Kempe, Bishop of London. This offer was accepted in 1461. Shortly afterwards he was appointed Dean of the Royal Chapel of St. Stephen, Westminster, April 29, 1462 ; while six years later, on the 16th of December, 1468 he was installed as prebend of Brownswood, in St. Paul's Cathedral, which he continued to hold until February 20, 1473, when he resigned, and was succeeded by Wm. Dudley, Dean of the Royal Chapel.

In 1470 he was appointed to be one of the Privy Council, and in the same year he was employed by his royal master upon an embassy to the King of Castile. Though we do not know how he behaved himself in this capacity, we must draw our own conclusions from the royal favours that were afterwards conferred upon him. He was appointed in 1471 to be one of the Privy Council, along with the Queen and others, to Edward, Prince of Wales, afterwards the ill-fated King Edward V., whom Richard III., to fulfil his own ambitious designs, ordered to be smothered in the tower : the Duke of York he also obtained by his craftiness, and the two brothers were murdered together, that Richard III. might have no one to molest his crown.

The same year as his appointment to the Privy Council of Edward, Prince of Wales, Edward IV., wishing to obtain the Scottish King for the help of the House of York, proposed a perpetual peace between the English and Scotch nations, and a marriage between the royal families. To further this momentous question he appointed commissioners to treat with the Scots, who likewise appointed commissioners. Amongst the English appears one ' doctor John Alcock.' These commissioners were appointed to meet at Alnwick on the 23rd of September, 1471, but from some reason, they did not assemble until the 25th of April,

1472, and then not at Alnwick, but at Newcastle-on-Tyne, when the treaty of peace was renewed.

As an illustration of the magnitude of these meetings, the Scottish Commissioners had passports for themselves (twelve) and four hundred attendants.

Some authorities say that Alcock was engaged with others in treating with the Commissioners of the Scottish King again in July, 1480, but I have found nothing to substantiate this statement.

By the transfer of Thos. Rotherham, Bishop of Rochester, to Lincoln, in 1472, the See became vacant. To this John Alcock was appointed as Rotherham's successor by Edward IV., from whom he obtained leave to be consecrated elsewhere than at Rochester, March 13, 1472. From a letter which still exists in Corpus College Library, Cambridge, we learn that Pope Paul II. exerted his influence with Edward IV. to have Alcock appointed Bishop of Rochester. But in what way had Alcock succeeded in obtaining the favour of Paul II. that he should thus write on his behalf? Those were not the days of messages delivered quick as lightning, as we now experience, and it shows that Alcock was renowned for something, either for his learning and piety, or his tact in negotiating, or his fame would not have reached so far from his own country.

In Corpus Library is another letter of this Pope. "*Epistola Papæ ad episcopum Norwicensem de eadem re. Hic notatur Joannem Alcock aliquamdiu suisse suffraganeum episcopi Norwicensis*" is the entry in Nasmyth's Catalogue.

During the first year of his bishopric he opened Parliament on the 16th of October, 1472, with the usual custom of a speech. He did this as deputy Lord Chancellor. Robert Stillington, Bishop of Bath and Wells, the Lord Chancellor, being ill and unable to attend to his duties, appointed him his deputy, and he was formally installed as deputy September 20, 1472 ; but upon his recovery, the Lord Chancellor prorogued the Parliament April 5, 1473, and resigned the seals of office to Lawrence Booth, the Bishop of Durham, his successor, June 8, following.

Not many years afterwards we come across the peculiar and unparalleled instance of two Lord Chancellors, Bishop Alcock being one. The circumstances under which this took place are these. Edward the IV., intending to invade France in the hope of gaining its crown, which invasion ended in the Peace of Pecquigny—he intended that the Lord Chancellor should accompany him as well as the Master of the Rolls, and other State office holders ; but finding it necessary to provide for the business of the Chancery in England, he nominated Bishop Alcock to take the duty in the Lord Chancellor's absence. Instead, however, of pursuing the customary practice of making him Keeper of the Seal only, he was invested and sworn in with the full power and title of Lord Chancellor of England, April, 27, 1475. From some cause the expedition was delayed from April to July, and during these three months Privy Seal bills were addressed to both officers in England, frequently on the same day and from the same place.

The last writ of the Privy Seal addressed to Bishop Alcock is dated September 28, 1475, after which, Bishop Rotherham—the Lord Chancellor—having returned, resumed his office. So Alcock was Lord Chancellor, jointly with Bishop Rotherham, from April to July, and alone from July to September, 1475. He was Lord Chancellor again in 1486, which will be described further on.

In 1476, at the request of John Dalton, an alderman of Hull, who had married his niece Katharine, he founded at Hull a Grammar School, which still exists. The Grammar School was pulled down in Edward the VI.'s reign, sold, and its revenues taken away, but they were afterwards restored, and the School rebuilt in exactly the same style as before ; it is still standing, but is not used as a School, a new School having been erected by its side. A history of this School was published by R. W. Corlass in 1878, to which I refer my readers for further particulars concerning the stipend of the master, that all were to be taught gratis.

In 1476 he was transferred to the See of Worcester, in succession to John Carpenter, who had resigned, but only survived his resignation a few months. The temporalities were given to him by the King, September 25th, 1476. During his bishopric he visited and restored the Church of Westbury. According to some authorities he was made Lord President of Wales, being the first occupant of that office, which he continued to hold for some time.

In 1471 he visited Little Malvern Priory, "rebuilt the church, repaired the convent, and in a great measure discharged their debts."

He caused a chapel to be built on the south side of Holy Trinity Church, Hull, and appointed a chanter "to pray for the souls of Edward VI., of himself, parents, and other relations, who were buried there, likewise for the souls of all Christians." This he built during 1478-83, possibly as a memorial to his brother and family, who were stricken of the plague in 1478.

At the battle of Bosworth Field Richard the III. was killed, and Henry the VII., the rightful heir, was restored to the throne. Before Richard III. proceeded to Bosworth, he took the seals away from John Russell, Bishop of London, and conferred them temporally upon Thomas Barrowe, the Master of the Rolls, for the despatch of necessary business. But Henry VII., immediately on his return to London, conferred the chancellorship upon Bishop Alcock, as being the person most fit to be trusted. The way in which he transacted the vexatious questions that were brought before him is described in Campbell's Lives of the Chancellors. He opened Parliament November 7, 1486, and declared the cause of the summons. The Chancellorship was taken from him and given to Thos. Morton, some time between August and November, 1487, not for any particular purpose, but that Henry might confer the honour upon one who had clung to his cause through thick and thin.

Bishop Alcock was transferred to the See of Ely by bill of provision, October 6, 1486. The royal assent was given, and the temporalities restored December 7. At that time the See of Ely was one of the richest in England.

St. Andrew's Day, 1489, witnessed the baptism of the Princess Margaret, afterwards Queen of Scots, Bishop Alcock officiating with others. A description of the ceremony is given in the "Antiquarian Repertory."

The relationship between the Bishop of Ely and the towns under his care was of the most amiable kind. In Cooper's Annals of Cambridge, there are records of gifts to him when he visited Cambridge.

The work by which his name will long be remembered, was his founding Jesus College, Cambridge, from the decayed nunnery of St. Rhadegund. This Nunnery had been founded over 300 years, but the nuns had gradually grown into disrepute, till at last it was "so that "their land lapsed for want of owners, or rather for the owners' want of honesty." Alcock petitioned the King and letters patent were issued to him June 12, 1497, to convert "the said Priory, or house, "into a college of one master, six fellows, and a certain number of "scholars, to be instructed in grammar, to pray and celebrate divine "offices within the college." Bishop Alcock's instrument of foundation bears the date December 9, 1497. The first statutes were given to the College by his successor, James Stanley, Bishop of Ely, after being confirmed by Pope Julius II. He did not end his work when he had obtained letters patent ; he built, or caused to be built, sufficient room for those whom the charter provided for.

Many of the palaces which then existed, were added to, rebuilt, or beautified in some manner during the time he was bishop ; and whatever he did he caused his crest to be placed thereon.

The Bishop died at Wisbeach Castle on the 1st of October, 1500, not long after the death of Archbishop Rotherham, a Yorkshireman like himself, whom Alcock came into contact with upon important occasions. He was buried in a chapel which he had built for himself in Ely Cathedral, and *not* taken to Hull as some authorities still erroneously say. This chapel he began to build in 1488, and shows the taste of the Bishop.

There are five books by Bishop Alcock, which were printed by Pynson and Wynkin de Worde.

I.   Spousage of the Virgin to Christ, 1446.
II. Mons Perfectionis. (1497.)
III. Gallicantus et Cofrates suos curatos in Sinodo apud Barnwell xxv. die mensis Septembris, 1498.
IV. Sermo Joh. Alcock, Episcopus Eliensis. N.D.
V.   The Abbaye of the Holy Ghost. N.D.

Cambridge, 1884.   G. J. GRAY.

PROFESSOR B.F. COCKER

THE subject of our sketch was born at Almondbury, Yorkshire, in the year 1821. His father designed him for one of the learned professions, and gave him the advantage of a good English education at King James's Grammar School, Almondbury, founded in 1609. Having a decided taste for business life, however, he was placed in a German business house (Huddersfield), where he laid the foundation of correct and methodical habits. He afterwards engaged in the manufacture of woollen goods, in which occupation he remained for seven years. In 1850 he was compelled, through failing health, to seek a change of climate. He determined on going to Australia, and, notwithstanding the misgivings of his friends as to the effect of a long sea voyage, he found himself, after the hardships and privations of a passage of sixteen weeks, immeasurably restored to health and vigour. He arrived at Launceston, where he remained about a year as the agent of an English shipping house. On the discovery of gold in Victoria, he removed to Melbourne, where he spent four years, carrying on a very large and successful mercantile business, engaging in the various benevolent and religious enterprises of that portion of the colony, and manifesting very marked ability, not only as a leading business man, but also in the various public affairs with which he became acquainted. The great panic of 1856, which involved nearly the entire colony in financial ruin, proved disastrous to his house, and after losing nearly all his apparently ample accumulation, he purchased a small vessel, and went on a trading voyage to New Zealand, Tonga, Fiji, and Tahiti. While in Fiji he visited the Wesleyan missionaries, and while on an excursion to the heathen temple, on one of the islands, he, with a companion, fell into the hands of the cannibals. Here his condition was, as may well be imagined, exceedingly uncomfortable. His fate, as well as that of his companion, seemed sealed ; the death song, which was to precede their being killed and devoured by the savages, had been already commenced, when, by the exercise of courage and the putting forth of an almost superhuman effort, they succeeded in breaking through the weakest part of the line, and escaping to their boat, whither they were pursued by the yelling horde, who were hungry for human flesh. After barely escaping the cannibals he had, on the same voyage, a narrow escape from shipwreck, but finally reached Australia in safety. On his return he effected an engagement as clerk in a lumber yard, where he continued for a time, after which he took the same vessel with which he had sailed to and from the scene of his adventure with the savages, and made for the Friendly Islands. He went ashore at Tonga, and sent the vessel on to Lakamba, one of the Fiji group, where she struck a reef, and went down immediately, the crew escaping. He again returned to Australia, and found employment as a wharfage clerk at Sydney for three months. It will thus be seen that his life had been for some time one of thrilling adventure, marked by marvellous escapes, and full of that varied and chequered experience which has been of the greatest practical utility to him in the years since intervening, and through which he has been fully qualified to sympathise with the tempest tossed child of affliction of whatever clime, or wherever found. Nor does the above brief recital of his trials, sufferings, and adversities end the chapter of strange and saddening circumstances which have enveloped the life history of this remarkable man. When his employment on the wharf at Sydney terminated, he started for Callas, and on the voyage encountered a shock

Professor Cocker.

of an earthquake, when about 400 miles from the South American coast. From Callas, by way of Panama and Aspinwall to New Orleans, thence up the Mississipi to Cairo, and from that point by rail to Chicago. His funds were now exhausted, and he endeavoured to find temporary employment at Chicago, but failed. Hearing of an old friend, who had as a southern missionary been the recipient of his bounty in Melbourne, and who now resided in Adrian, Michigan, he immediately started for that point. A beloved child died on the journey, and he found himself landed in Adrian with one child dead in his arms, three living, but these helpless, children and a wife depending on him for support, while he was absolutely penniless. This was in 1857. In Adrian he found generous friends who aided him in his distress, and the presiding elder of that district in the Detroit Conference, appointed him as pastor of the Methodist Episcopal Church in the little village of Palmyra. He remained in this charge nearly two years, and so warmly were the people attached to him that the Presbyterians of that locality attended his services, and aided in his support. At this point he was cheered by the friendship of many worthy men, among whom may be mentioned the late Judge Tiffany, a legal author of note, Hon. G. C. Harvey, and others, who recognised his ability and predicted for him no ordinary future. From Palmyra to Adrian, Ypsilanti, Ann Arbor, thence again to Adrian, back to Ann Arbor, remaining in every charge as long as the economy of his church would permit, and securing the respect and confidence of every community in which he lived and laboured. His character, preaching, labours, and administration were never either questioned or criticised by his people. In fact, the esteem in which he was held was universal with all classes of good citizens; his popularity would have spoiled a man of less sense. In the annual conference his opinions were always treated with the greatest consideration, while leading divines of national reputation sought his acquaintance in the general conference of the church in which he has been a representative. At the conference of 1869 he was appointed to the pastorate of the Central M. E. Church, in the city of Detroit, which, however, he resigned in a few weeks, to the great regret of his parishoners, to take the chair of mental and moral philosophy in the University of Michigan, to which he had been elected in September, 1869, and which he filled at the time of his death. Before his connection with the University his contributions on metaphysical and also on general literary and scientific subjects to the *Methodist Quarterly* and other journals, had attracted favourable notice. In 1870 he published "Christianity and Greek Philosophy;" in 1873, "Lectures on the Truth of the Christian Religion;" and in 1875, "Theist Conception of the World." These works have been warmly received by eminent scholars, and have been noticed in the most flattering manner by literary journals in this country and in Europe. The style of the distinguished author was one of rare beauty. While firm in the expression of his opinions, and fearless in defending his positions, yet he maintained the utmost courtesy to all opponents. His writings stamped him as a man of scholarly attainments, wide and familiar acquaintance with scientific research, large mental vigour, and a polish and refinement on a par with the highest culture of this age. He had, at the time of his death, in process of preparation a "Handbook of Philosophy," and a work on "Materialism." The Wesleyan University conferred on him the degree of M.A. in 1864; Asbury College, D.D.; and he was still further recognised by receiving the degree of LL.D., from Victoria College, Ontario, in 1874. While occupying his position in the University, he performed a large amount of work as a Christian minister.

In appearance Dr. Cocker was intellectual and venerable. Genial as a warm hearted boy, he was grave in appearance, and treated with cheerfulness, though with dignity and seriousness, the great problems of the here and hereafter. He appeared aged for his years, in physical appearance he was at once unpretending and striking. Nearly six feet high, of a rather slight build, a strong face, a large, kindly, penetrating, dark eye ; the whole countenance indicating one admirable blending of strength and benevolence. The hair, once dark, was white, and very abundant, covering a large and firmly formed head. He was, in the best sense of the term, a noble man. The doctor leaves an estimable wife, who for years has been the companion of his strange and chequered life, and who has during all these years kindly, tenderly, and lovingly cared for him in his physical feebleness. He has also two sons surviving of a family of seven children. Both are graduates of the University. The oldest. William J.. is now, and has been for some years, superintendent of the Adrian High school. Henry R., is connected with a business in St. Paul's, Minnesota. The labours of Dr. Cocker will appear the more extraordinary when we consider that he had all through life laboured under physical disabilities, often involving intense suffering, which would have utterly crushed a man of less will power.

BISHOP PURSGLOVE

BISHOP Pursglove was born at Tideswell, and " brought up by parents care at schoole, and learning trade." His uncle, William Bradshawe, of London, then took him and placed him in St. Paul's School, where he remained at that uncle's cost and charge for nine years. From there he was removed to the Priory of St. Mary Overy, in Southwark, now known as St. Saviour's, Southwark. This Priory was surrendered to Henry VIII. in October, 1539, so that it must have been before that time that Pursglove was there. From St. Mary Overy, he proceeded to Oxford, where he remained for fourteen years, and became " a clerk of learning great." From the University, Pursglove went to Guisborough Abbey, in Yorkshire, where he was made Prior on the 1st of July, 1519, and so remained till the dissolution of that House in 1540, a period of twenty-one years. Pursglove is said to have been sufficiently alive to his own interests at the time to have been officiously ready and willing to do the King's bidding. He " acted as Commissioner for the King in the inquiries into other Priories, and persuading the Abbots and others to resign their houses." For the obsequiousness to the ruling powers he was rewarded with a pension— very large in those days—of £166 13s. 4d. per annum. Of the minute details of his monastic life, and the manner in which he fulfilled his duties during a stormy and dangerous period, we have no record. That his merit and talent were conspicuous, appeared from his rapid promotion, "being consecrated Bishop Suffragan of Hull in the beginning of Queen Mary's reign, and also appointed Archdeacon of Nottingham. But although he slackened in zeal for the Reformation during Queen Mary's time, and joined the Conformists, yet afterwards,

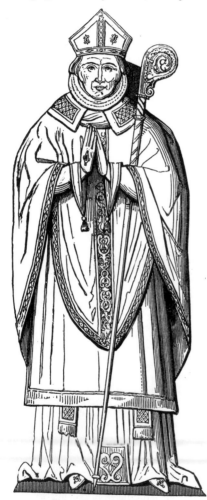

Brass of Bishop Pursglove.

in the second year of Queen Elizabeth's reign, A.D. 1559, when "all spiritual persons holding preferment were required to take the oath of supremacy" he, along with all the other Bishops excepting Kitchen, of Llandaff, gave up his dignities and preferments, rather than acknowledge any Head or Governor of the Church, excepting only one Lord and Saviour Jesus Christ."

On giving up his preferments and dignities in 1559, Bishop Pursglove appears to have retired to his native village Tideswell, and to have thenceforth busied himself in good works both there and at Guisborough. In 1560 he founded under letters patent, the "Grammar School of Jesus," at Tideswell, which he endowed with certain lands for future maintenance. The deed of foundation is a model of preciseness in laying down every minute detail connected with its management. It was incorporated and had a Common Seal. The Seal is oval in form, and bears beneath a canopy a somewhat rudely executed draped figure of our Saviour, the head surrounded by a nimbus, and the hands uplifted; the right hand having the finger extended in the conventional form of benediction, and the left holding the orb and cross. It bears the inscription SIGILLO - COE - SCOLE GRAMATICALIS DE - IFSI - DE - TYDW'L.

In 1561, Pursglove founded a somewhat similar but more extensive charity at Guisborough, in Cleveland, which was called " The Hospital and School of Jesus at Guisburne." The Ordinances for the government

Seal of Guisboro' School.   Seal of Tideswell School.

of the School are almost identical with those of Tideswell. The seal is of oval form, and bears a not very artistic figure of our Saviour beneath a rude canopy, both hands are raised, and in the left the figure, which

Norman Gateway, Guisbro' Priory.

is draped to the feet, holds an orb and cross. Beneath the feet is the sun surrounded by rays. It bears the inscription SIGILLR - COE - SCOLE - SIVE - HOSPITALIS - IESV - DE - GISBVR.

Bishop Pursglove died full of years, and with the consciousness of having done much good in his generation at his native place, on the 2nd of May, 1579, and was buried in the grand old Parish Church of Tideswell. A remarkably fine and interesting monumental brass preserves, not only his memory, but his features and personal appearance in full episcopal robes. The figure, which is three feet five inches in height, represents the Bishop full length, with mitre and crozier. Beneath the figure is a square brass plate bearing the following inscription. It is engraved in black letter and Roman capital letters, and is as follows :—

Under this stone as here doth Ly A corps sometime of fame
in tiddeswall bred and born truely, ROBERT PURSGLOVE by name
and there brought up by parents care at Schoole & learning trad
till afterwards by UNCLE dear to London he was had
who WILLIAM BRADSHAW hight by name in pauls wch did him place
and yr at Schoole did him maintain full thrice 3 whole years space
and then into the Abberye ye was placed as I wish
in Southwarke call'd where it doth Ly Saint MARY OVERIS
to OXFORD then who did him Send into that Colledge right
And there 14 years did him find, wh Corpus Christi hight
From thence at length away he went, A Clerke of learning great
to GISBURN ABBEY Streight was sent and placd in PRIORS seat
BISHOP of HULL he was also ARCHDEACON of NOTTINGHAM
PROVOST of RoTHERAM COLLEDGE too, of YORK eak SUFFRAGAN
two GRAMER Schooles he did ordain with Land for to Endure
one HOSPITAL for to maintain twelbe impotent and poor
O GISBURNE thou with TIDDESWALL TOWN Lement & mourn you may
for this said CLERK of great renown Lyeth here compast in clay
though cruell DEATH hath now dow' brought this BODY we here doth ly
yet trump of FAME Stay can he nought to Sound his praise on high
Qui legis hunc bersum crebo reliquum memoreris
bile cadaber Sum tuque cadaber e. ris.

The slab in which this figure and inscription are inserted, is surrounded by a border-line of brass, bearing an inscription, and at the corners are the four emblems of the Evangelists. The inscription, which is in old English lettering, is as follows :—

" +Christ is to me as life on earth, and death to me is gaine
Because I trust through him alone salvation to obtaine
So brittle is the state of man, so soon it doth decay,
So all the glory of this world must pass and fade away.
This Robert Pursglove sometyme Bishoppe of Hull deceassed the 2 day
of Maii in the yere of our Lord God 1579."

" The Hollies," Duffield, Derby.   LLEWELLYNN JEWITT, F.S.A.

BISHOP BRIAN WALTON

It is rather a remarkable circumstance, that three of the greatest Biblical scholars whom this country has produced should have sprung from about the centre of Cleveland, viz., Bishop Brian Walton, D.D., the Rev. John Mawer, D.D., and the Rev. John Oxlee, "the Star of the West." Brian Walton was born at Seamer, two miles N.W. from Stokesley, about the year 1600. As the parish register of Seamer does

Brian Walton, D.D.

not commence until 1638, (when Walton was rector of Sandon, in Essex, and had been for twelve years rector of St. Martin's Orgar, in London), it is useless to search it for the baptism of this learned divine; but that there were Waltons residing at Seamer when Brian, at the age af thirty-five, was officiatiñg as a clergyman in London, is proved by the following hitherto unpublished entry, which I have copied from the register of the adjoining chapelry of Middleton-on-Leven :—"Willm. Walton, of Seamer, Clerk, and Isabell Boult, were married the fifth day of September, anno domini 1635."

In July, 1616, three months after the death of Shakspere, Brian Walton, was admitted a Sizar of Magdalene College, Cambridge, and was removed to Peter House, in the same university, also as a Sizar, December 4th, 1618. In 1619, he took the degree of Bachelor of Arts, and in 1623, that of Master. Leaving Cambridge, he became, for a short time, a curate and schoolmaster in Suffolk, and afterwards assistant curate at the church of All Hallows, Bread Street, London. In 1626, he was appointed rector of St. Martin's Orgar, in Cannon Street, London, where he was soon "over head and ears" in one of those unfortunate quarrels about tithes, which have so often been a cause of alienation between the clergy of established churches and the souls committed to their cure.

On the fifteenth of January, 1635-6, he was instituted to the two rectories of St. Giles-in-the-Fields, London, and of Sandon, in Essex, but for some cause or other, he did not long retain the former of those benefices, but continued to hold that of St. Martin's Orgar. He is suppcsed also at this time to have been one of the chaplains to Charles the First and a prebendary of St. Paul's Cathedral. In 1640, when May was merry with her blossoms and her flowers, the heart of the learned Brian Walton was sad, for the shadow of Death had overspread his Essex rectory, and he was no more to be comforted in this life by the dear wife of his bosom—one of the Claxtons of Suffolk. He was incorporated Doctor of Divinity, at Oxford, August 12th, 1645, as noticed in Anthony a Wood's *Fasti Oxonienses*, and *not* in 1660, as some writers mis-state. He had, indeed, "commenced Doctor in Divinity," at Cambridge, in 1639, but had been driven from the university, like many others, by the revolutionary hurricane that swept over the land. Having already had a chancery suit with his parishioners of St. Martin's Orgar, regarding tithes, we find him, in 1641, charged by them before Parliament with sundry offences ; such as insisting on, and, by his own hands, placing the communion-table under the east window ; reading one part of the morning service at the reading-desk, and the other part at the communion-table ; not preaching on Sunday afternoons, nor allowing the parishioners to procure a lecturer at their own charge ; that he was non-resident all the summer, and committed "the charge of the petitioners' souls to an ignorant curate, maintaining him no otherwise than with a salary catched out of the revenue of the parish lands ;" and that, to use the language of the petition, "he disgracefully and contemptuously asperseth those persons of quality and worth, which at this time serve the Commonwealth in the honourable house of Parliament, as men chosen for the knights and burgesses of this city ; affirming that the city had chosen Soame, because he would not pay ship-money ; Vassal, because he would not pay the king his customs ; Pennington, because he entertains silenced ministers ; and Cradocke to send them over into New England ;" and they besought Parliament "to examine their abuses, and to take some course for their reformation." The end of all this was, that Walton is *supposed* to have been dispossessed of both his rectories ; that, towards the latter end of 1642, he was according to WALKER's *Sufferings of the Clergy*, "sent for into custody as a delinquent." The same author informs us, that once, when sought for by a party of horse sent in pursuit of him, he hid himself amongst the broom,—the pretty emblem of the old Plantagenets. Devoting himself to upholding the King's prerogative against Parliament, Walton retired to Oxford, until the royal cause became hopeless ; upon which he returned to London, taking up his abode in St. Giles, Cripplegate Churchyard, in the house of Dr. William Fuller, whose daughter, Jane, he had married for his second wife. From thence he issued, in 1652, his " Brief Description of an Edition of the Bible, in the original Hebrew, Samaritan, and Greek, with the most ancient translations of the Jewish and Christian Churches, viz. : the Sept. Greek, Chaldee, Syriac, Ethiopic, Arabic, Persian, etc., and the Latin Versions of them all : a new Apparatus," etc. The Council of State, by their order bearing date Sunday, July 11th, 1652, gave their approbation and allowance of the work, declaring the same to be "very honourable and deserving of encouragement." Archbishop Usher and John Seldon, two of the most eminent scholars of the day, published their testimonial to the merits of the work, as "more useful than any that hath been hitherto published in that kind; and that the printing thereof will conduce much to the glory of God, and the public honour of our nation;" and begging of the learned to give it "all due encouragement;" an appeal that was heartily responded to, notwithstanding the troubles of the times, for by May 4th, 1652, the handsome sum of £9,000 was promised for the work. The first volume of the Polyglot, containing the Pentateuch, was sent to the press in the Autumn of 1653, and delivered to the subscribers in 1654, and the whole six volumes completed in 1657. In the first Latin preface to the Polyglot, Dr. Walton acknowledged his obligations for the charter granted by the Commonwealth's-men for exempting the book from paper duty, "and afterwards kindly confirmed and continued by His Serene Highness the Lord Protector in Council for the purpose of furthering the work."

When a new English translation of the Bible was contemplated by the "Grand Committee of Religion," January 16th. 1656-7, we learn from BULSTRODE WHITELOCKE, Lord Commissioner of the Great Seal to Cromwell, that Dr. Walton was the first named to be consulted on the subject.

Soon after the Restoration, Dr. Walton was appointed chaplain to the king; and, on the second of December, 1660, he was consecrated in Westminster Abbey as Bishop of Chester. In March, 1661, we find him one of the Commissioners at the Savoy Conference. In September of the same year, he visited Chester, entering the ancient city on Wednesday, the eleventh of that month, amidst a great display of swords and firelocks, not much in keeping with Christianity; for the whole militia of the city and county were assembled, to salute him with vollies of shot, and five troops of horse had met him overnight at Nantwich, to escort him to his See; and there was much firing of gunpowder, and eating and drinking in thorough English fashion. But short was the learned Doctor's enjoyment of his new honour; for, returning from Chester to London, he fell sick, and died at his house in Aldersgate Street, November 29th, 1661; and, on the fifth of December following, was interred with much pomp in the south aisle of St. Paul's Cathedral.

Stokesley.   GEORGE MARKHAM TWEDDELL.

JOHN WYCLIFFE

THE years which commenced with 1877, and will end with 1884, mark the five hundredth anniversaries of the culminating events of Wycliffe's life; for it was in the year 1377 that Wycliffe was made the butt of five Papal Bulls addressed severally to the King, the Parliament, the University, the Primate, and the Bishop of London; his chief crime being that of having translated and diffused, through his loyal

Lollards, the sacred Scriptures, long so jealously guarded from the people by the successors of those apostles who were commissioned to preach the Gospel to every creature. And it was on the 29th of December, 1384, that, upon the altar-steps of his parish church of Lutterworth, during the celebration of the Mass, and just as the host was about to be uplifted, paralysis struck down the illustrious celebrant, in presence of the people, and the New Year's morning of 1385 rose upon John Wycliffe dead and peaceful in his bed, instead of charred and blackened by the martyr flame.

There are many biographies which would give more interest to the seeker after excitement, and the lover of mere romance; for, being devoted to one fixed and sublime object, the life of Wycliffe was wanting in that diversity of incident and restlessness of movement from which biography derives a superficial charm. But its steady and dauntless consecration to that one high aim gives to the life itself a glory which is not to be found in the more fitful glamour of an orbit less concentric, or a purpose less intense.

Not only was Wycliffe the "Morning star of the Reformation," but he was the intellectual and spiritual luminary of the times in which he lived. At the beginning of the fourteenth century the depth and

John Wycliffe. From Portrait in the Rectory, Wycliffe.

density of popular ignorance were extreme. Not only was the Bible little known, and slenderly appreciated, but perfunctory teaching in the schools, and ineffective ministrations from the pulpit, did little or nothing to raise the curtain from the public mind. The personal corruption of the priesthood was only to be paralleled by their official ambition. Hence, with the blind leading the blind, both priest and people lapsed down a declivity of moral degradation, and wallowed together in a gulf of religious darkness and pollution.

It was upon times like these that the orb of Wycliffe's life arose. Born in the little village of Wicklif, about six miles from Richmond, in Yorkshire, from a family tainted with the religious superstition of the age, he became separated from their home and even from their name. Tradition says that his ancestors claimed to be lords of the manor from the Conquest, and that at the beginning of the seventeenth century the marriage of the heiress caused the property to pass to a family of another name   But John de Wycliffe evidently took his name from his birthplace, not from his parents, and, either disowned by them because of aspiration, or breaking away from them because of their superstitions, he prosecuted his independent studies, and supported himself by his own energy.   Nothing authentic concerning his childhood or his schooldays has come down to us.   There is reason to conjecture that it was not in any monastic institution that the first germs of his studies were fostered.   The monopoly which the cloister had long held in learning and tuition was beginning to be broken, and local schools, conducted with rare ability, were scattered through the land.   In one of these we may suppose Wycliffe received the qualification to enter Queen's College, Oxford, which he did at the age of seventeen; subsequently, however, exchanging it for Merton College, where, a few years before, Bradwardine had fulminated his philippics on " The Cause of God against Pelagius."

Knighton, a writer who hated Wycliffe and his views, makes this testimony concerning the young student's aptitude and success in learning :—In philosophia nulli reputabatur secundis ; in scholasticis disciplinis incomparabilis."*

If it is true, as has been said, that the philosophy of Aristotle was the only key by which the treasures of revealed theology could be unlocked, Wycliffe lost no time in appropriating that key, for he committed to memory many of the more intricate sections of Aristotle's writings.   His study of the Bible itself was pursued with a kind of spiritual voracity which indicates his hunger after the highest truth. But it called for the highest courage of the embryo Reformer to withstand the fashionable distaste to Scriptural exercitation, and use the Bible as his text-book instead of the sentences and compilations of men.   Friar Bacon says : " the graduate who reads or keeps the text of Scripture is compelled to give way to the reader of the sentences, who everywhere enjoys honour and precedence.   He who reads the sentences has the choice of his hour, and ample entertainment among the religious orders.   He who reads the Bible is destitute of these advantages, and sues, like a mendicant, for the use of such hours as it may please them to grant.   He who reads the sums of Divinity is everywhere allowed to hold disputations, and is venerated as a master ; he who only reads the text is not permitted to dispute at all, which is absurd."   To this testimony Le Bas, in his Life of Wycliffe, p. 78,

---

* Knighton De Eventibus Angliæ, cal. 2644.

adds, " The Biblical method of instruction was trampled under foot by the overbearing authority of irrefragable and seraphic doctors. And yet, in this state of the public mind it was that Wycliffe ventured to associate the study of the Scriptures with the keenest pursuit of the scholastic metaphysics, and to assign to the Bible the full supremacy which belongs to it, as disclosing to us the Way, the Truth, and the Life."

Through the variety of his attainments, and chiefly by the profundity of his Biblical knowledge, Wycliffe rose to the high dignity of Evangelical or Gospel doctor, because he was "mighty in the Scriptures."

Stirred to its depths by the shock of the great and devastating Plague, in 1347, the spiritual nature of the Reformer began to kindle with his intellectual power, and a stirring little tract, entitled " The Last Age of the Church," was penned by him when he was 32 years of age, in 1356.   In this tract he fell in with the popular superstition which interpreted the Plague as the precursor of the final judgment; and, like many less worthy prophets of a later time, he fixed the date of the close of the fourteenth century as the end of the history of the world.   He based this prediction on carefully and learnedly calculated data, and on no mere hectic superstition.   Cabalistic computations founded on hieroglyphic forms, on the letters of the Hebrew alphabet, coupled with some imaginary hints or administrations of Scripture, impelled him, amid the solemn excitement of the crisis, to commit himself to these vaticinations.   His career as a Reformer may be said to have commenced at this point.   Withdrawing from public observation for a season, he re-appeared to wage a stern controversy with the mendicants, or begging friars.   During the twenty years covering the period from 1360 to 1380, Wycliffe maintained his battle with this sanctimonious order, whose history and pretensions we have no space here to trace.   In the latter of these years he published his " Objections to the Friars," in the conclusion of which he says : "The fryars have been cause, beginnge, and maintaininge of purturbation in Christendom, and of all evils of this worlde.   These errors shall never be amended till fryars be brought to freedom of the Gospel, and clean religion of Jesus Christ."   When he was sick, and supposed to be dying, a deputation from the friars visited him, and urged him to recant his errors; he beckoned to his attendant to lift him in his bed, and calling up all his strength he cried aloud, " I will not die but live, and shall again declare the evil deeds of the friars."

Appointed to the lucrative position of Warden in Canterbury Hall, attempts were so persistently made to dispossess him that he made his appeal to the Pope, who transferred the decision to one of his cardinals. It was kept in abeyance until a further controversy arose, not very dissimilar in its main lines of disputation from one provoked a few years ago between Mr. Gladstone and Father (now Cardinal) Newman, on the issue of the Vatican decrees by the Æcumenical Council of 1874, and which involved the grave question of the civil allegiance, and traversed the central claim of the temporal power of Popes. Edward, after conferring on Wycliffe the rank and dignity of royal chaplain, was fickle and contemptible enough to deprive him of his post of Warden of Baliol. Occupying the divinity chair at Oxford, it was either whilst he was abroad in Bruges, or immediately on his return, in 1376, that he was appointed rector of Lutterworth, in Leicestershire. Whether he resigned his chair in Oxford is not known ; but he spent nearly all

John Wiclif, from Balels "Centuries of British Writers" (1548.)

his time in his midland rectory, devoting himself to the work of a country pastor, and a translator of the Scriptures.

The civil war which followed on the accession of Richard II., arose out of the luxury and simony of the Pope and prelates. And this served to make fresh occasion for the Reformer's zeal. There is no need to attempt here to lend dramatic feature to his appearance in St. Paul's before the assembled prelates, as he boldly vindicated his views, and denounced the corruptions of the Church. Escaping from the rigours of an ordeal which his successors would have shortened into an abrupt appeal from the hierarch to the headsman, he retreated to his Leicestershire benefice, where he preached the Gospel with a fervour and an influence which soon became contagious, and yearning for some potent engine, like the printing-press, to diffuse the words of life as he transcribed them, he trained his hero band of Lollards, whose diligent and faithful pens made duplicates and copies of the priceless manuscript, and who read and taught its truths by the light they gathered from their master. It was the increase in the number, and the boldness, and the influence of these Lollards which seemed to fan the spirit of persecution into the flame which glowed around the army of the martyrs who were fast mustering in a devoted conscription.

Wycliffe lived to see at least some of his followers suffer persecution. But, like the Hebrew youths of old, the fire leaped around himself but did not burn him. Before the time of the Reformer, and before the blood of John Huss and Jerome of Prague had sealed their testimony, the consecrated Waldenses had borne faithful witness for the truth. From the summit of the Piedmont Alps the witness was forthcoming from free and hardy mountaineers. The home of the glacier was the pulpit of the Gospel. And from the valleys below, the voices of the Albigenses and the descendants of the Vaudois, rang forth a faithful echo. But while simpler and less subtle witnesses were called to the sacrifice of liberty and life in the cause to which they were committed, the learning and the might of Wycliffe were exerted in the same high behoof with a comparative impunity. Whether it was policy, or conscience, or the love of letters which gained noble patronage and protection for the Lutterworth Reformer we cannot say ; but, certain it is, that although living, as it were, in a den of lions, with the espionage of Rome as vigilant, and her ferocity as keen as ever, the mouths of the beasts which gnashed around him were divinely stopped. Precluded by weakness from appearing as often and as

Wycliffe, Yorkshire.

regularly as formerly in his pulpit before his people, Wycliffe still wielded his pen for liberty of conscience and free religion in his Leicestershire study to the last. A special occasion would still find him in his church taking his part in the public celebrations. And Christmas of 1384 found him at the various Masses of that high festival. The 29th of December fell upon a Sunday, and the Rector of Lutterworth was at the altar. Old in work and care, though not in years, paralysis seized upon him, and he dropped down before the people, just as the Host was being raised ; and two days afterwards, at 60 years of age, he died.

But if he was thus permitted to pass away naturally, instead of by the stake, the air grew dark with vultures who made carrion of his good name. Scurrility and abuse poured forth from ribald pulpits and from bigot altars; and the death throes into which paralysis had thrown him were publicly proclaimed to be the curse of God, and bishops told their flocks that he had "breathed out his malicious spirit to the abodes of darkness."

And as the taste of blood began to grow familiar with the horrors of the martyr age; as the split of the faggot grew into a familiar sound, and the shriek of the tortured fell into a hackneyed tune, the thirst for vengeance, hitherto impotent and frenzied, gathered strength. The birds of prey were darkening the ecclesiastical sky, and in 1415, thirty years after John Wycliffe's death, they gathered thick and fierce in the Council of Constance. Here the writings of the Reformer were arraigned and branded with the mark of heresy, and the memory of their author handed over to infamy and execration; and the following edict was decreed: "That his body and bones, if they might be discovered, and known from the bodies of other faithful people, should be taken from the ground, and thrown away from the burial of any church, according to the canon laws and decrees." Thirteen years after the issuing of this decree, the hawks wheeled and poised their evil wings over the green mounds of the Lutterworth graveyard; and swooping down on what they imagined was the resting-place of Wycliffe, the greedy talons crooked under the daisy roots; the vault was opened, ransacked, and despoiled; the ashes that were found were rudely burned, and then scattered on the fleet ripples of the brooklet called the Swift, which babbled near; these ripplets carried them to the Avon, the Avon to the Severn, the Severn to the sea. Thus did the Lollards take from Wycliffe's pen the record he translated; the faithful took them from the Lollards; the printing press, in the next century, took them from the faithful, and floated the truth into the sea of human heart and home-life through the world.

Birmingham.   ARTHUR MURSELL.

ANDREW MARVELL

F there is one name in the long roll of Yorkshire Worthies, great and famous as a vast number of these have been, of which Yorkshiremen may feel justly proud, it is that of Andrew Marvell,—a poet of no mean ability—a brilliant wit and keen satirist, conspicuous even amongst the Rochesters, Sedleys, and Buckinghams of the court of Charles the Second; a statesman of acute perception, and above all, a pure-minded patriot in the most corrupt times. His life occupied an eventful period, that of the struggle of Charles the First with the Parliament, resulting in the Civil War and the decapitation of the King; the Protectorate of Cromwell and the reign of the Puritans; and the restoration and reign of the second Charles, with its profligacy and licentiousness, in strange contrast to the piety and fanaticism of the preceding decade.

The Rev. Andrew Marvell, his father, was a native of Meldrith, in Cambridgeshire, and became Rector of Winestead, in Holderness, in 1614, resigning the living in 1624 on his appointment to the Lectureship of Holy Trinity, Hull; he was also Head Master of the Grammar School in the same town, which office he held in 1620. He was drowned when crossing the Humber in 1640, leaving issue, by Anne, daughter of —— Pease, whom he married in 1612, at Cherry Burton, near Beverley, Andrew, his only son; Anne, who married Jas. Blaydes, from whom are descended the Thompsons, the Haworths, the Schonswars, and other notable Hull families; and Maria, who married Edward Popple, from whom are the Popples, of Welton, near Hull.

Andrew the younger was born at Winestead, in 1621, not at Hull, as is frequently stated. He was educated at his father's school, whence he proceeded, at the age of 15, to Cambridge, and graduated

B.A. in 1638, attracting considerable attention by his facility in learning and superiority in mental power. At this time the Jesuits who were ever on the outlook for young men of promise, heard reports of his talent, sought him out; by their persuasive eloquence induced him to listen to their teachings, and eventually inveigled him to London, with a view of going to Douay, to study for their priesthood. His father hearing of this, followed him to London, found out where he was staying, and persuaded him to return to Cambridge, where he remained until his father's death terminated his college career

On his return to Hull, he was adopted by Mrs. Skinner, of Thornton, in Lincolnshire, a lady of competent fortune, whose only daughter had perished along with his father. The young lady had been on a visit to the Marvells, and persisted in crossing the Humber in a storm, despite the advice of the boatmen and of Mr. Marvell, in order that her mother might not be disquieted by her not returning at the promised time. Marvell therefore resolved to share the peril, and both were drowned. At her death Mrs. Skinner left all her property to her adopted son.

Andrew Marvell.

About the year 1642 he made a continental tour through Holland, France, Spain, and Italy, meeting with Milton in Rome, where a life-lasting friendship was commenced. After his return, he became, in 1650, tutor to Mary, daughter of Thos. Lord Fairfax, the great Parliamentarian General, who afterwards married the profligate Geo. Villiers, Duke of Buckingham. He was a devoted admirer of Fairfax, and whilst in his establishment wrote two poems, one on "Nun Appleton," the other on "Bilborough" the seats of his lordship.

Four years afterwards Cromwell gave him the appointment of Preceptor to his nephew, Dutton; and in 1657 that of Latin Secretary under Milton, for foreign affairs. He had been recommended to the office in 1652, by Milton, in a letter to President Bradshaw, wherein he says :—" He hath spent four years abroad to very good purpose, as I believe, and the gaining of four languages. Besides, he is a scholar and well read in Latin and Greek authors ; and no doubt of an approved conversation, for he comes, now lately, out of the house of the Lord Fairfax, who was Generall, where he was entrusted to give some instruction, in the languages, to the lady, his daughter, ... It would be hard to find a man so fit, every way, for that purpose, etc." The letter, however, failed in procuring the office for him at that time.

He was chosen to represent Hull in the short Parliament (1658) of the Protectorate of Richard Cromwell, and again in the 1st of Charles II. (1660). At that time there were no newspapers to give information of the debates, but Marvell sent down to his constituents a resumé of the proceedings, these letters occupying 400 pages in Thompson's edition of his works.

In 1661 he went to Holland, when Lord Belasyse, High Steward of Hull, suggested the expediency of electing a new member in his place ; but Marvell receiving notice of this, returned, and obtained the assent of his constituents to a further absence, to go with the Earl of Carlisle on his embassy to Russia, Denmark, and Sweden, and he remained their representative until his death. There is no evidence to shew that he ever spoke in the House, but he attended assiduously to his duties, and took copious notes of the debates for transmission to Hull.

As a statesman he ever exhibited a conscientious integrity, and that at a time when conscience had very little to do with politics, place hunting, and sinecures ; and the court was one mass of corruption. An anecdote is told of a later period which is an apt illustration of this. Lord Stair, in an interview with Caroline, Queen of George II., spoke of his conscience in connection with some matter of politics, when the Queen said, " Ah, my Lord, ne me parler point de conscience, vous me faites évanouir."

There is a well-known story told of him that Danby, the Lord Treasurer, desiring to bribe him to support the Government, found him in an obscure lodging, and hinted that the King, conscious of his merit, desired to present him with £1,000 in acknowledgment thereof, upon which Marvell called up his serving boy, and told him to shew his Lordship the mutton bones intended for his dinner, adding, " Such being the smallness of my necessities, I require not the gift," and politely bowed the courtier out. Pitt said " Every man has his own price ; I know of but one exception, and that is Marvell, in the past." Despite his legacy from Mrs. Skinner, so slender were his means when he died, notwithstanding his opportunities of acquiring wealth by venality, that the Corporation of Hull voted a sum of money to pay his funeral expenses.

The most famous of his controversies was with Dr. Parker, in defence of Nonconformity. Dr Parker, originally a Puritan, now " in ritualism a Pharisee, in life a Publican," whom Marvell described as " a maggot transformed into a carrion fly," had written a preface to a work by Archbishop Bramhall (1672) in which he warmly condemned the Nonconformists. Marvell replied to it in " The Rehearsal Transposed," respecting which Burnet said, " Parker had entertained the nation with several virulent works, and was attacked by the liveliest droll of the age, who wrote in a burlesque strain, but with so peculiar and entertaining a conduct, that, down from the King to the tradesman, his book was read with pleasure," and that " he not only humbled Parker but the whole party, for the author of ' The Rehearsal Transposed' had all the men of wit on his side." And Swift said that this was " the only instance of an answer, which could be read with pleasure, when the publication which occasioned it was forgotten." Parker is said to have cut so ridiculous a figure in the controversy, that even his friends could not forbear laughing at him. The Doctor replied in " The Reproof of the Rehearsal Transposed," wherein he urged the Government " to

Marvell's House, Highgate—Front View.

suppress the pestilent wit, the servant of Cromwell, and the friend of Milton." Marvell then came out with " The Rehearsal Transposed, the second part," to which he was partly incited, by an " Epistle " signed " F. G." in defence of Parker, which concluded with—" If thou darest to print any lie or libel against Dr. Parker, I will cut thy throat." To the second part of " The Rehearsal " Parker made no response, thinking perhaps, that with " so pestilent a wit," " discretion was the better part of valour."

Dr. Croft, Bishop of Hereford, in 1674, published " The Naked Truth, or the true state of the Primitive Church; by a Humble Moderator," in advocacy of toleration and charity in matters of religion;

which was attacked by Dr. Francis Turner, in "Animadversions on 'The Naked Truth, etc.'" To this Marvell replied in satirical style, in "Mr Smirke, or the Divine in mode, etc." together with a short historical essay concerning General Councils, etc., a work which displayed great erudition and vivacity of style.

The last controversial work was "A Defence of John Howe, whose Tract on Divine Prescience has been rudely attacked by his opponents, 1677"; a work that is now very scarce, not having been included in any collected edition of Marvell's works.

His last work of importance was "The Growth of Popery, 1678," in which he vindicates the principles of the English Constitution, and discusses, with great freedom, the limits of the Royal Prerogative. It was published anonymously, and proved to be so bitter a pill to the advocates of "Divine Right of Kings," that a reward of £100 was offered for the discovery of the author. One of his chief opponents was

Marvell's House—Back View.

L'Estrange, the paid advocate of High Church principles, and arbitrary government, who attempted to write him down, but was no match in wit for the supporter of liberty, although the latter had to write under the disadvantage of penalties and imprisonment hanging over him.

In the later period of his life he published many satires and *jeu-d'esprit*, notably one on the King's speeches, which he produced, with much pungent wit. His intrepid defence of civil and religious liberty, raised up for him a host of enemies in the court circle, and he was frequently obliged to conceal himself from those who sought to maltreat and even kill him. It has even been asserted that he eventually fell a prey to their machinations, and that his death was occasioned by a dose of poison secretly administered to him. He died in the year 1678, and was buried in the Church of St. Giles in the Fields, London.

Portraits of him by A. Hauseman, Gasper, Smith, and Thurston, all in private hands, were exhibited at South Kensington, in 1866, and two at Leeds, in 1868. There is one in the British Museum, and another in the Trinity House, Hull, many of which have been engraved, those by Hauseman and Smith, by the Arundel Society.

Two statues have been executed by Keyworth, jun., Hull, one for the Public Park, and the other for the Town Hall, Hull.

The life of Marvell has been written by W. Cooke, 1772; Captain Thompson, 1776; John Dove, in Hartley Coleridge's "Yorkshire Worthies," 1835; John Symons, in "Hullinia," 1872; Reginald Corlass, in "Hull Authors," 1879; and in all Encyclopædias, Biographical Dictionaries, etc., as well as in a multitude of journals, English, American, and European.

LIST OF MARVELL'S WORKS.

"The Works of A. M.; to which is prefixed an account of the Life and Writings of the Author. By Mr. Cooke. 2 vols. London, 1772."

This edition contains only the Poems and Letters. Reprinted, 1773; with Portrait.

"The Works of A. M., Esq.; Poetical, Controversial, and Political. Containing many original Letters, Poems, and Tracts never before printed. With a new life of the Author. By Captain Edward Thompson (of Hull). Portrait by Basire, London, 1776."

"Life of A. M., the celebrated Patriot with extracts and selections from his Prose and Poetical Works. By John Dove, London, 1832."

"The Poetical Works of A. M.; with a Memoir of the Author. Boston, Mass., 1857."

"The Poetical Works of A. M., M.P. for Hull, 1868; with Memoir of the Author. London, 1870."

"The complete Works, in Verse and Prose, of A. M., M.P.; for the first time collected and collated with the originals and early editions, and considerably enlarged with hitherto un-edited Prose, and Poems, and Translations of the Greek and Latin Poetry; and, in quarto form, an original Portrait on steel, other Portraits, fac-similes, and illustrations. Edited, with memorial introduction and notes, by the Rev. Alex. B. Grosart, St. George's, Blackburn. 4 vols. For private circulation only. Vol. 1, 1872."

"The Poetical Works of A. M.; with a memoir of the Author. London, 1881."

"A. M. in London, with a view of his residence there. 'Art Journal.' 1849, p. 85."

"Flecknoe; an English Priest, circa 1642. A humourous satire, written in Rome."

"Satirical Verses, in Latin, on Launcelot Joseph de Maniban, an Abbé and Fortune Teller, Circa 1642. Written in Paris."

"The Rehearsal Transposed; or Animadversions upon a late work entituled, ' A Preface, shewing what grounds there are of fears and jealousies of Popery,' by Dr. Samuel Parker, Bishop of Oxford. London, 1672-3. Second edition, 1673. Replied to in ' Gregory Father Greybeard with his vizard off, etc,' 1672, and "A Reproof to the Rehearsal Transposed,' 1673."

"The Rehearsal Transposed; the second part occasioned by two letters:—the first printed by a nameless author (Bishop Parker) entitled ' A Reproof to the Rehearsal, etc.'; the second a letter left for me at a friend's house, subscribed J. G. 1673."

"Mr. Smirke, or, the Divine in mode; being certain annotations upon the Animadversions on 'The Naked Truth' (by Dr. Parker). London, 1676, 1680, and 1689."

"An Account of the growth of Popery and Arbitrary Government in England, more particularly from the long prorogation of Parliament of November, 1675, ending the 18th of February, 1676, till the last meeting of Parliament the 16th July 1677. Amsterdam, 1677. London, 1678. Reprinted in 'State Tracts,' 1689. A reward of £100 was offered by the Government for the discovery of the author-ship. In reply, appeared "The Parallel; or an account of the growth of knavery under the pretext of Arbitrary Government and Popery, etc. By Sir R. L'Estrange. London, 1679.'"

"Remarks upon a Discourse, writ by one T. D., under the pretence of answering Mr. G. Howe's letter . . of 'God's Prescience.'" By a Protestant. London, 1678.

"Advice to a Printer; a Satire, 1678."

"Miscellaneous Poems, London, 1681. Portrait by Cipriani."

"A short Historical Essay on General Councils, Creeds, and Impostures in matters of Religion; very seasonable at these times. London, 1687."

"A Collection of Poems on Affairs of State. By A. M. and other wits; the second part by A. M. ; the third part by Esquire Marvell."

"Further Instructions to a Printer, and the late Lord Rochester's Funeral. London, 1689 and 1703."

"The Lives of the 12 Cæsars, by Setonius Tranquillus, done into English by several hands, with a Life of the Author, and notes, by A. M. London, 1670, 1672. 1677, 1688."

"The Royal Manual; a Poem supposed to have been written by A. M., and now first published. London, 1751."

"A reasonable Argument to persuade all the Grand Juries of England to petition for a Parliament. Printed in Cobbett's 'Parliamentary History, vol. 4, 1806.'"

"Flagellum Parliamentarium; being sarcastic notices of nearly 200 members of the first Parliament after the Restoration, A.D. 1661 to 1678. Edited by Sir Harris Nicolas, from a contemporary MS. in the British Museum, London, 1827."

This work (by A. M.) was originally published with some variations, under the title of "A Seasonable Argument," 1806. Another copy, also in the British Museum, was printed with the title of "A List of the Principal Labourers in the design of Popery, etc." Reprinted by the Aungerville Society in "Reprints of scarce Tracts." A reward of £50 was offered by the Government for the discovery of the writer.

Five hymns and paraphrases, including "The spacious firmament on high," which appeared in "The Spectator," were claimed for Marvell by Captain Thompson, on the ground that he had seen them in a MS. book of his; but Jas. Montgomery, in a lecture at Hull, disputed this, from internal evidence, the hymns not being at all in the style of Marvell or of the 17th century, but quite in that of Addison and the post Revolution writers; adding that it was usual for persons of literary taste to make transcripts of poetry that struck them; and further that the MS. book referred to was not Marvell's, but more recent by a considerable length of time.

London.   FREDK. ROSS.

THE END.

WILLIAM STERNDALE BENNETT

SIR WILLIAM STERNDALE BENNETT, Professor of Music at the University of Cambridge, and Mus. Doc. of Oxford, was unquestionably one of the most distinguished musicians England has produced for a century and a half, and is the only Englishman who since Purcell has made a great reputation throughout the musical world of the Continent as well as his own country.

Sir W. S. Bennett's compositions are studied, played, and sung wherever musical students, players, and singers are to be found. His published compositions form, however, but a portion of the work by which he has fairly entitled himself to the respect of his countrymen and the mark of favour bestowed upon him by his Sovereign. Throughout his life he was a preacher and a prophet in the art, giving freely his time and his talent wherever they seemed likely to be useful for good. The resuscitation of the Royal Academy of Music, which had arrived at the verge of extinction, was a service which, while it only could have been possible to a man of special position and genius, would have been undertaken by few in the face of the difficulties and discouragements incident to the task. While Principal of the Royal Academy of Music, he was also one of its earliest pupils. He was born at Sheffield, where his father, an excellent musician, was organist of the principal church. Having lost both his parents in his infancy, he was brought up by his grandfather, John Bennett, one of the lay clerks of the Cambridge University choir, by whom he was entered when eight years old as a chorister of King's College, Cambridge. Here he remained two years, and was then placed in the Royal Academy of Music in London. He began his regular musical studies by taking the violin as his instrument, but he soon abandoned it for the pianoforte, upon which he received instruction from Mr. Holmes and Mr. Cipriani Potter. Soon afterwards he turned his attention to composition, and, as a pupil of Dr. Crotch, produced his first symphony in E flat at the Royal Academy, which was followed at short intervals by his pianoforte concertos in D minor, E flat, C minor, F minor (two), and A minor, which, with the exception of the first, were performed by invitation at the concerts of the Philharmonic Society. He became acquainted with Mendelssohn during one of that distinguished composer's visits to London, and by his invitation followed him to Leipzig, to enjoy the benefit of his instructions in harmony. Until the death of the great

Sir W. S. Bennett.

artist, Dr. Bennett was on terms of the most intimate friendship with him, and the influence of Mendelssohn's style is clearly shown in Dr. Bennett's compositions. During his sojourn in Leipzig, in the years 1837 and 1838, he, through Mendelssohn's influence, had the honour of executing a pianoforte concerto of his own composition at one of the celebrated Gewandhaus concerts, and later several of his works (amongst others his overtures to the "Naiades" and the "Wood Nymph," and his concertos in C and F. minor) were peformed before the same critical audience. He remained some years in Germany, and many of his principal compositions were published there and received

126

with great favour by the critics and the public. He finally fixed his residence in London, where he obtained a deservedly high position as a composer, a performer, and a teacher of music, and in 1856 he was appointed to succeed Mr. Walmsley as professor of music at the University of Cambridge. He obtained the degree of Doctor of Music in the same year, and of M.A. in 1869, and was also created D.C.L. of the University of Oxford in 187C. Professor Bennett succeeded Professor Wagner as conductor of the Philharmonic concerts in 1856, held that post until 1868, when he was appointed principal of the Royal Academy of Music. At the opening of the International Exhibition, 1862, Dr. Bennett was invited, in conjunction with Auber, Meyerbeer, and Verdi, to compose a piece of music to Tennyson's Ode, "Uplift a thousand voices," written expressly for the occasion. In the next month he composed the music to the ode by Professor Charles Kingsley on the installation of the Duke of Devonshire as Chancellor of the University of Cambridge, and this composition was immediately followed by his production of his fantasia-overture "Paradise and the Peri," written for the jubilee concert of the Philharmonic Society.

Sir W. S. Bennett's published works are numerous, including his overtures to the "Naiades," "The Wood Nymph," "Parisina," and the "Merry Wives of Windsor," concertos, sonatas, studies for the piano-fortes, songs, duets, and other vocal pieces. His "May Queen," produced at the first Leeds Musical Festival, in 1858, is probably the best known of his vocal compositions. For several years he occupied the position of Principal of the Royal Academy of Music, to which he was devotedly attached, and his able defence of which at the time it was proposed to withdraw the annual Government grant of £500 will be vividly remembered. It may be truthfully said that to his influence and powerful efforts England is at this time indebted for the existence of that most valuable educational institution. Dr. Bennett's high talents and the services rendered to his country were recognised by Her Majesty, and he received the honour of knighthood, at Windsor, in 1871. He died Feb. 1st, 1875, and was interred in Westminster Abbey.

WILLIAM JACKSON

In a far away north-west corner of Yorkshire, at the foot of one of its loveliest valleys, Wensleydale, stands the little town of Masham. Its few houses are clustered about the square grass-grown market place, which is only filled once a year, when a great sheep fair is held. Except on that special occasion, the small place is as sleepy and dull as could well be imagined. Perhaps one should say was, for quite recently a railway has been made by the North-Eastern Railway Company, connecting Masham with its main line at Ripon, and this has of course brought it a little more into connection with the outer world. Masham is beautifully situated by the river Yore, or Ure, surrounded on all sides by well wooded country and fine sweeping moorlands.

In this sequestered spot was born, on the 9th of January, 1816, William Jackson the musician. Nature is usually supposed to influence poets more often than musicians, yet nothing but nature and an inherited love of music can have been William Jackson's inspiration. He was far removed from any opportunity of hearing the works of the great masters, and for years he had to content himself with studying their compositions in score before he could hear their wonderful effects in performance. He walked all the distance between Masham and York to hear an oratorio which was performed in York Minster when he was a boy of fifteen or sixteen.

His father carried on the business of a corn miller at Masham, and he himself worked both in the mill and on the farm attached to it. His ruling passion, the love of music, revealed itself when he was very young. When he was about eight years old there was a great bell-ringing match at Masham, which gave him much pleasurable excitement. The music he heard in church on Sundays also fascinated him. It was produced by a large barrel-organ, the doors of which were thrown open behind to admit the sound into the church, and from the gallery the little boy used to watch with great delight the mysterious stops, pipes, keyboards, and all the machinery which was then exposed to view. His first musical instrument was an old fife, which his father had played with the Masham Volunteers. This fife, however, would not sound D, and so was not altogether satisfactory; but his mother encouraged his attempts by giving him a one-keyed flute, and shortly after he was presented with a flute with four silver keys; after that he piped away to his heart's content.

He first went to a school at Tanfield, where he very quickly proved himself to be an apt scholar by disputing with the old master on a question of grammar. After some natural hesitation the master found himself in the wrong, and, on admitting it, calmly told Jackson to take the grammar class himself for the future. His parents felt that it was high time their son should receive more education than that, and sent him to a boarding-school at Pateley Bridge, where they hoped he would study something more than music. Here he soon found congenial society in a club of village singers, who taught him to read music, in which art he soon became proficient, and astonished his comrades by his rapid progress. On his return home he was ambitious to make an organ, and, after repeated efforts, with his father's help he succeeded in constructing one which was the source of admiration and amazement to the country side. Not satisfied with this achievement, he immediately set to work to produce a finger-organ. After many failures, and as the result of much patience and perseverance, he at last became the happy possessor of an organ on which he could play, an old harpsichord which his father possessed supplying the keyboard.

During this period some sheets of Boyce's cathedral music were given to him, and he also procured Calcott's Grammar of Thorough Bass. These were of immense help to him in increasing his knowledge of harmony ; he mastered the Grammar very thoroughly, and so laid the foundation of his correctness in musical composition. His first attempts in this direction were some little anthems, which were submitted as the work of a boy of fourteen to Mr. Camidge, organist of York Minster, who kindly pointed out incorrect passages, and pronounced the favourable verdict that they did the boy credit, and he must go on writing. About this time a military band was formed in Masham, which the youthful musician joined. He not only wrote music which the band performed, but played every instrument in turn, always supplying the place of an absent member. · In this manner he acquired a very accurate knowledge of the capabilities and effects of each instrument in the wind orchestra. He also taught himself to play the violin and other stringed instruments, though he did not become a brilliant performer. All this practical knowledge was of enormous benefit to him when he began to write his scores for oratorios and other important works. When young Jackson was sixteen years old the lord of the manor presented a new organ to the church to replace the now worn-out barrel-organ, and Jackson was appointed organist at a salary of £30 a year. This was great encouragement to the young student, who thenceforth devoted all his spare moments to the study of music in one form or another. By means of a circulating library at Leeds he was enabled to borrow the works of Handel, Mozart, Haydn, etc., and, when possible, he always procured the full scores. He now began to give lessons in music, but was often discouraged by the want of promise in his pupils. Parents, too, were ignorant and unreasonable. One lady observed to him on bringing a pupil—"My daughter, you see, is a very good scholar ; she reads, writes, and counts, and I think if she had a quarter's music and a quarter's French she would be quite *top't* out." Teaching therefore was neither very pleasant nor very profitable, and Jackson had to take to other less congenial means of earning his bread.

In 1839 he published his first anthem, " For joy let cheerful valleys sing," and the following year his well-known glee, " The Sisters of the Sea," won the first prize offered by the Huddersfield Glee Club for an original composition. In addition to these and many minor works, he wrote during this period of his life his great work, " The Deliverance of Israel from Babylon," the last chorus being completed on his 29th birthday. There is no doubt that this is Mr. Jackson's masterpiece, and, remembering the few advantages the composer had then enjoyed —how he had altogether educated himself musically, and the difficulties under which it was produced—it must be admitted that this work is a remarkable testimony to the genius of its author. This oratorio was first performed in the Music Hall, Leeds, on May 25th, 1847. A local notice of the performance says—" The Deliverance comes to us an oratorio conceived and completed without the advantage of a single trial, even of the vocal score alone, much less of those rich orchestral effects which Mr. Jackson himself (equally with the audience) heard for the first time on Tuesday last. In awarding the due meed of praise to Mr. Jackson this circumstance must not be forgotten, though the oratorio needs no mention of it as an apology." A little later he wrote a second oratorio, the " Isaiah," which was published in 1851. Mr. Jackson's literary labours were not altogether confined to writing music ; he contributed a series of articles, called " Rambles in York-shire," to a local paper, and wrote and delivered several lectures to various societies.

In 1852 he left the scene of his youthful successes and took up his abode in the stirring growing town of Bradford. Here he was appointed conductor of the Bradford Festival Choral Society at its foundation, and he held that appointment until his death. In this capacity he trained hundreds of voices, and developed a love of choral singing amongst the people of Bradford which they yet gratefully remember, and tell with pride of the time when Mr. Jackson was invited to take his choir to Buckingham Palace to sing before Her Majesty Queen Victoria. Amongst the many duties of his busy life, his organ and other appointments, his business as music seller, and his teaching, he still found time for composition. In 1856 he wrote music to the 103rd Psalm, which was performed at the Bradford Musical Festival of that year; and for the succeeding festival, 1859, his cantata " The Year " was written. He also brought out a book of Psalm tunes for peculiar metres, many of them of singular beauty. His " Singing Class Manual " is still a standard book for class singing in large schools. A church service, a mass, and several anthems, glees, and part songs were also the production of his busy brain. Mr. Jackson's compara-tively early death, on April 15th, 1866, after a very short illness, was a great blow not only to the wife and children who survived him, but also to a great number of warmly attached friends, for his was one of those natures whom to know was to esteem and love. It was said of him that " he was essentially a genius, and he had a keen appreciation of humour and ' airy nothings ' if clothed in beautiful attire, but he was free from the vices and blemishes which are supposed to be the natural inheritance of genius. What he set himself to do he did with indomi-table perseverance and patience, and he was never satisfied till he had fully acquired what he aimed at. His desire for knowledge was omnivorous, and he was one of the best informed men of the town of Bradford on matters of science, art, and literature. From the nature of his engagements and associations he was necessarily exposed to great temptations, but through them all he walked unscathed, and by his example and admonitions he succeeded in raising the standard of morals in the musical profession of the neighbourhood. He was a man of spotless integrity, of great generosity, and liberal-mindedness."

During the whole time of his connection with the Bradford Festival Choral Society his services were gratuitous, and his fellow-townsmen, in consideration of his generous work, and as a mark of their esteem and respect, spontaneously subscribed the sum of £2,000, which was invested for the benefit of his widow and young children. The Choral Society supplemented this by their own special expression of affection in a memorial stone which was erected in the Undercliffe Cemetery, and the people of his native town (Masham) erected a similar token of their regard in the churchyard there.

The following lines were written by one of his friends on hearing of his death :—

IN MEMORIAM.

Some lives best speak for themselves ; words are ours ;
Alas ! they are the coins we give and take—
Poor counterfeits that oft we pass for deeds.
He whom we mourn to-day as a lost friend,
A sober manliness of speech was his,—
A soul attuned to high and noble aims,
Battling huge disadvantage bravely down,
Winning respect and love from many hearts.
The music of his soul he gave to us,
Which through the years shall live and bless our lives,
And to the sense of beauty in the soul
Whisper delightful cadences of sound.
So is he not for ever lost to us,
But still in blest association lives
For ever in our midst, a spirit pure,
Whose legacy to earth enriches its
Inheritance of heaven.   W. H.

Mr. Jackson's eldest surviving son, also called William Jackson, who was born at Bradford in 1853, was a young man of great promise, who inherited not only his father's admirable qualities, but also his love of music. He studied music at the Conservatoire in Stuttgart, was an excellent organist, and received an appointment in Edinburgh. He wrote some clever and original little musical works, but his early death, at the age of twenty-four, cut short his very promising career before he had been allowed to give to the world the results of his studies.

London, April, 1884.   S. UNWIN

JOHN JACKSON

JOHN JACKSON, the eminent portrait painter, was born at Lastingham, Yorkshire, in 1778, and died in 1831. The following anecdotes concerning him are taken from "The Life of the Rev. Robert Newton, D.D., Wesleyan Minister":—Among Newton's acquaintances in early life was John Jackson, who afterwards became one of the most distinguished artists of his age, and member of the Royal Academy. He was the son of a village tailor, and for a time followed his father's occupation—making and repairing garments for the farmers and peasantry in that part of Yorkshire. Yet, even then, the love of art predominated in his mind, and he not unfrequently attempted to sketch the features of his friend Robert. One of these early efforts of his pencil is still preserved in the family, and is said to be an excellent likeness. Nobody then suspected the eminence to which these two country lads would attain by the force of their own talents and genius. Jackson's abilities were called forth under the patronage of an English nobleman; the latent powers of young Newton were developed under the influence of Methodism. When Jackson was in the height of his popularity in London as a portrait painter, his friend Newton, who was equally distinguished as a public speaker, often remarked that he had once coaxed the young artist to make him a waistcoat; and when they met, as they frequently did, the incidents connected with their boyish intercourse were to them a source of endless amusement. Jackson was once engaged to paint a full-length portrait of the Duke of Wellington for some public institution, when a difference of opinion arose between them as to the attitude in which his Grace should stand; and, as the Duke had long been accustomed to command, he would have his own way in this case, and the artist, for the time, was compelled to submit. He succeeded, however, in drawing the Duke into an agreeable conversation, so that he became bland and free; and then, with admirable tact, he said, "Your grace will excuse me, but the attitude which you have chosen is exactly that of a drill-sergeant." This observation put an end to the dispute. Without offering another word of objection, the great general assumed the position which the artist recommended. It was not befitting for the conqueror of Bonaparte to appear as a subaltern; and Jackson was pleased to think that he had overcome the hero of a hundred battles.

T. W.

THOMAS PROCTOR

THOMAS PROCTOR, a very promising artist, and one of the earliest sculptors of the English school, was born at Settle in 1753, being the son of an innkeeper, and was educated at the Giggleswick Grammar School. At the age of 18 he went to London, and became a clerk in a merchant's office, but feeling that art was his vocation, he became a student of the Royal Academy, and studied both as a painter and sculptor for about three years. He received a medal for a drawing of a figure in chalk, and another for a model in clay of an Academy figure ; and, in 1784, he won the gold medal for an historical picture, the subject being taken from Shakespeare's "Tempest." He also received medals from the Society of Arts. When Proctor gained the prize, his enthusiastic fellow-students hoisted him on their shoulders and bore him in triumph round the quadrangle of Somerset House, shouting out " Proctor, Proctor !" Barry was delighted at this, and cried " That's right, boys ; the Greeks did it—the old Greeks did it." The genius of the young Yorkshireman developed fast—Barry and West both thought highly of him—but at the termination of his academical studies he was penniless and ill. Mr. West had arranged to send him to Rome as a travelling student ; he went to his native home to arrange for the payment of his debts and for his visit to Italy. On his return he caught cold, which soon ended in consumption, from which he soon after died in obscure lodgings in Clare Market in 1794. He was buried in Hampstead churchyard. Sir Abraham Hume purchased his chief works, " Ixion on the Wheel," and " Prometheus ;" but another very fine group, representing " Diomedes and his Horses," he could not sell and destroyed, as it was too large to be placed in his cellar. Proctor was unquestionably an artist of great genius, but he lived, unfortunately, at a time when art was not appreciated. He was patronised by a few discerning minds, but was of too proud and independent a spirit to accept what he did not give an equivalent for, and his short career presents a mournful contrast to the princely fortunes made by clever artists of our time.

Swaledale.   R. V. TAYLOR, B.A.

WILLIAM LODGE

WILLIAM LODGE was born at Leeds in 1649, the son of William Lodge, a Leeds merchant, by Elizabeth, daughter of John Sykes, and grand-daughter of Richard Sykes, the first Alderman of Leeds, and died at Leeds in 1689. He was educated to the legal profession, but inheriting an estate of £300 per annum, he abandoned law, and devoted himself to sketching and engraving, more for amusement and a love of art than for profit. He accompanied Lord Belasyse on his Embassy to Venice, where he met with Barri's " Viaggio Pittoresco," of which he published a translation, illustrated with portraits, in 1679. On his return he engraved shells and fossils for Dr. Martin Lister's " Illustra-tions of Natural History" in the " Transactions of the Royal Society." He became a member of the York Club of Virtuosi, where he made the acquaintance of Francis Place, whom he accompanied on a sketching excursion, in the course of which he was apprehended as a Jesuit in disguise, and cast into prison at Chester, as one of the Popish plotters denounced by Titus Oates. Thoresby relates that he had a dream that he was dead and buried in Harewood churchyard, which vexed him, as he wished to lie by his mother at Gisbourn, and he gave special directions in his will that he should be buried at the latter place. Accordingly, when he did die, his body was placed in a hearse for conveyance to Gisbourn, but in passing through Harewood the hearse broke down and the coffin burst open, the corpse rolling out into the road. As the hearse could not proceed, the coffin was hastily patched together and deposited in a grave in Harewood churchyard, and there I believe it still remains. (See Jones's " History of Harewood.") The following list comprises the more important of his engravings — Etchings of heads for the "Viaggio Pittoresco ;" views of towns for Thoresby's "Ducatus Leodiensis ;" York, from the Manor House to the Water House; views of Leeds, Wakefield, Alnwick, Tynemouth Castle, Holy Island, Berwick, Carlisle, Edinburgh, Glasgow, Barnard Castle, Sheriff Hutton Castle, Kirkstall and Fountains Abbeys, Westminster Hall and Abbey, Lambeth Palace, Gaeta, the Mole and Plaucus's Tomb, Pozzuolo, Baiæ, Caracalla's Mole ; Oliver Cromwell and his Page, dedicated to the Protector, &c. His own portrait is given in Walpole's " Engravers," and another, engraved by Barrett, has been published. Whether Edmund Lodge is descended from the Lodges of Leeds I cannot say, but it seems to be not improbable, as there were several of the name in the town in the 17th century. A Rev. Mr. Lodge was Incumbent of St. John's, Leeds, in 1709, and in 1713 Thoresby speaks of attending the funeral of " Mr. Thomas, a younger son of the late Mr. Lodge." The above William Lodge gave two of the eight bells to the Parish Church of Leeds.

London.   F. Ross.

TITUS SALT

A YORKSHIRE MERCHANT PRINCE.

Sir Titus Salt, Bart., was born at the Old Manor House, Morley, near Leeds, on the 20th of September, 1803. The house is well designated " old," for it was built more than three hundred years ago,

Manor House, Morley, birthplace of Sir Titus Salt, Bart.

and must have been a substantial building when first erected. The walls are in some places three feet thick; the roof is low and covered with grey slates. The kitchen still retains many of its antique features, having its stone flags, the ceiling with its bare wooden beams, where the oat-cakes were suspended to harden, and the hams to dry. Sir

Titus was the first of a large family, consisting of three sons and four daughters, all of whom are gone. In olden times a Manor was attached to the house, but all traces of the manorial acres have disappeared, or undergone a transformation.

Mr. Daniel Salt, his father, was, at the time his son was born, engaged in the business of an ironmonger, and highly respected in the village. But finding that business did not realise his expectations, he removed when his son was a few years old, to a farm at Crofton, near Wakefield, and subsequently to Bradford, where he commenced the business of a woolstapler. Master Salt was in due time sent to school, and subsequently taken into the warehouse to assist his father. Whatever deficiency there may have been in his early training was well supplied by the more effective discipline of self-education. Having acquainted himself with the routine of the warehouse, he was sent to learn the worsted spinning business; and when this was acquired he commenced, with his father, the manufacture of worsted goods. He endeavoured to introduce new improvements into that branch of industry, and was very successful; but it was not till a later period that he found the article with which his speculative mind was afterwards so much absorbed, and which in a great measure laid the foundation of his future success.

It was during the existence of the partnership with his father that Sir Titus introduced into the worsted trade a kind of fibre called Russian Donskoi Wool. He, soon after this discovery, went into business on his own account. On one of his ordinary business journeys to Liverpool, in 1836, he first became acquainted with the material with which his fame is now associated,—Alpaca Wool. A large quantity of that material had been imported from the Brazils and was stored in Liverpool. But the rats appear to have been the only parties who approved at all of the importation; yet, notwithstanding the unfavourable opinion of the material which some people held, Sir Titus proceeded to buy up all the Alpaca to be found in Liverpool; eventually established the manufacture; and laid the foundation of a princely fortune. Thus was he the originator of a new and important branch of industry, which became, during his lifetime, a permanent staple trade, adding to the comforts and luxuries of our race, and giving employment to thousands. In a few years Alpaca cloth was known and valued all the world over. After carrying on the manufacture for many years, Mr. Salt thought of retiring from business, but before his fiftieth birthday came, on which he intended to retire, he determined on account of his five sons to continue a little longer at the head of the firm. Thus fully decided, he resolved to leave the overcrowded town of Bradford, and in 1851 commenced the erection of his great model factory and workmen's town, Saltaire.

In the strictest sense of the word Sir Titus Salt was a philanthropist. We can but briefly enumerate in our limited space a few of his munificent acts. Not only has he surrounded his noble palaces of industry at Saltaire with dwellings which are models of elegance, comfort, and sanitation (resembling in this regard the mill itself), but he has also provided other comforts and even luxuries for his workpeople. He has erected baths and washhouses with every desirable appliance. There are 45 almshouses, with a weekly allowance for the maintenance of their inmates, and to these there is a neat little chapel attached. A magnificent Congregational Chapel, in the Italian style of architecture, was built entirely at his expense, (at a cost of £16,000), which is fitted up and decorated with the most exquisite taste and refinement. He built the Saltaire Factory Schools, in a style of which it has been said

Arms of Sir Titus Salt., Bart.

that "whatever art could invent or money buy, has been brought together here." The building, which accommodates 750 children, stands back sixty feet from the roadway, with an ornamental garden between the tasteful palisade and the school. Two of the lions originally intended for the Nelson Monument, in London, are placed on pedestals at the extremities of the palisade, and opposite them are the corresponding pair flanking the palisade enclosing the Saltaire Club and Institute,- -another of Sir Titus's gifts to the town, built at a cost of £18,366. It is said that there is no public building in the United Kingdom so richly decorated. Sir Titus Salt prohibited public-houses in Saltaire, but gave this noble institution as a substitute. "It is intended to supply the advantages of a public-house without its evils. It will be a place of resort for conversation, business, recreation, and refreshment, as well as for education, elementary, technical, and scientific." On the north side of the town, and on both banks of the river, is situated Saltaire Park, another of his gifts. It covers fourteen acres, has a cricket-ground and boat-house, and is laid out in a very tasteful manner. He also erected a Sunday School, capable of holding 1,000 children, the foundation-stone of which was laid by two of his grandsons, in May, 1875. Other places have had experience of his generosity. He gave £5,000 to the Bradford Fever Hospital, £5,000 to the Lancaster Lunatic Asylum, £1,000 towards the Peel Park, Bradford, and a wing to the Hull Orphan Asylum.

Sir Titus Salt was Chief Constable of Bradford before the incorporation of that borough, and afterwards, in 1848-9, he was Mayor.

In 1859 he was returned by the Liberal party M.P. for Bradford, but retired in 1861. In October, 1869, Her Majesty conferred upon him, in recognition of his varied merits and services as a loyal citizen, an eminent manufacturer, a generous master, and an enlightened philanthropist, the distinction of a baronetcy. Other and not less gratifying marks of esteem he has received from his workpeople and

Sir Titus Salt, Bart., J.P., D.L.

neighbours. Three years after the opening of the Saltaire works, he was presented with a magnificent bust in the finest Carrara marble, standing on a shaft and pedestal of Sicilian marble, and in 1871 (by 2,296 subscribers) with his portrait, which is deposited in the Institute at Saltaire.

On Saturday, the 1st of August, 1874, a splendid statue of Sir Titus Salt, erected in front of the Bradford Town Hall, was unveiled by the Duke of Devonshire, in presence of a large number of spectators.

Nearly £3,000 had been raised for the purpose by a public subscription, in sums varying from five shillings to a *maximum* of £5. Sir Titus had scruples against the erection of such a memorial in his lifetime, but his objections were overcome, and the statue was completed within four years after the first suggestion of the idea.

Sir Titus married, in 1829, Caroline, daughter of George Whitlam, Esq., of Great Grimsby, and had a numerous family. He died on the 29th of December, 1876, at his favourite residence, Crow Nest, near Halifax, and his remains are deposited in the family mausoleum at Saltaire.

Morley, near Leeds.   THE EDITOR.

JOHN GOWER

EARLY three centuries have passed away since Ben Jonson was appointed to the office of Poet Laureate by Royal Letters Patent, but the office was of still more ancient origin, for Jonson had many predecessors, who were styled Volunteer Laureates. Amongst these were men of eminence, such as Chaucer, Spencer, and others, and the list further contains the name of a Yorkshireman, Sir John Gower, who was born about 1320, and was of good family, had wealth and social position. He was a member of the Inner Temple, and Leland says that "Gower was made Chief Justice of the Court of Common Pleas," but this is doubtful. Richard II., meeting Gower rowing on the Thames, near London, invited him into the royal barge, and after much conversation, requested him to "book some new things." The poet complied, and composed the "Lover's Confession," which was printed by Caxton in 1483. Gower died in 1402. He went totally blind some years before his death. He was buried in St. Mary Overy, Southwark. The office of Poet Laureate is one possessing many features of interest. Its antiquity, royal connection, historical uses, the literary celebrity of those who have held the office, and its curious privileges, and also the rewards connected with it, including the title, salary, and butt of wine,— all these might furnish matter for a readable chapter in English history. The purpose, however, of this notice is to call attention to one of the poets who held the office of Poet Laureate by kingly favour. Amongst the fourteen poets who have thus been honoured since the days of Johnson, we find the name of one Yorkshireman, the Rev. Laurence Eusden, of whom it is said—

> Eusden, a laurell'd Bard, by fortune rais'd,
> By very few been read, by fewer praised.

Eusden was born at Spofforth, as the following entry in the parish register will shew :—

1688. Laurence, ye son of Dr. Eusden, the rector of Spofforth, was baptised the 6th day of September.

He was educated at Trinity College, Cambridge, and was afterwards for some time chaplain to Lord Willoughby de Broke, through whose interest he received the living of Coningsby in Lincolnshire. His poems are now quite forgotten, and were held in little esteem during his lifetime. He did no honour to Yorkshire, for he was a sycophant of no ordinary type, as seen in his adulatory poems on his friends and odes to the King, in which excess of flattery is the most noticeable feature. A critic, Mr. Oldmixon, in his "Arts of Logic and Rhetoric," says of Eusden—"The putting of the laurel on the head of one who writ such verses will give futurity a very lively idea of the judgment and justice of those who bestowed it. For of all the galimatias I ever met with none comes up to some of the verses of this poet, which have as much of the ridiculum and the fustian in them as can well be jumbled together; and are of that sort of nonsense which so perfectly confounds all ideas, that there is no distinct one left in the mind." The compositions of Eusden could scarcely fail to evoke ridicule, and in the *Grub Street Journal* (Aug. 27th, 1730), there appeared the following parody of Dryden's celebrated epigram on Milton; our Yorkshire Poet Laureate is the hero :—

> Three poets (grave divines) in England born,
> The Prince's entry did with verse adorn,
> The first in lowliness of thought surpassed;
> The next in bombast; and in both the last.
> Dullness no more could for her Laureate do.
> To perfect him, she joined the former two.

The appointment of Eusden as Poet Laureate gave John Sheffield, Duke of Buckingham, the topic for his famous little satirical poem, called "The Election of a Poet Laureate." The Duke describes the rushing in of the poets who were anxious for the honour, and tells how the god Apollo is bewildered by the clamour of the assembled candidates, eager for the crown, when—

> At last rushed in Eusden, and cried, "Who shall have it,
> But I, the true laureat, to whom the King gave it ?"
> Apollo begged pardon, and granted his claim,
> But vowed that till then he had ne'er heard his name.

His excesses in drink put an end to Eusden's life, on the 27th of September, 1730. Gray said of him "That he was a person of great hopes in his youth, though at last he turned out a drunken parson." Our Yorkshire Poet Laureate was succeeded in the office by Colley Cibber, actor, playwright, and hero of the "Dunciad."

Morley, near Leeds.   THE EDITOR.

ROBERT COLLYER

THE Rev. Robert Collyer is known to large numbers of people in Yorkshire, and throughout the country by all Unitarians, as one of the foremost preachers in America. Mr. Collyer's life has been almost a romance, in the development of the eloquent preacher from the Yorkshire blacksmith ; born December 8th, 1823, at Keighley, though his parents lived at Blubberhouses before and shortly after his birth, the embryo preacher's early environments were cast in a pretty country village, which his memory continues to cherish with the fondest love. Surrounded by the rich-coloured heather-clad moors, and within a short distance of the lovely woods of Bolton, the young student passed the early years of his life, and, gifted with a mind to see and feel the

Robert Collyer.

beauties of nature, an indelible mark was made on his character through these associations, to which constantly-recurring allusions in his writings testify. He received little schooling, his education under the village pedagogue beginning when he was four years of age, and lasting just the same number of years. But his education was not allowed to finish with attendance at school, for the little he had there learned merely served as an incentive to self-exertion in the acquisition of further knowledge.

Of Mr. Collyer's feeling towards the land of his birth and his ancestry, we cannot do better than quote the following remarks taken from a speech delivered by him in London in 1871 :—"There has never been a moment in the 21 years that I have been absent from this land when it has not been one of the proudest recollections that I came of this old English stock ; that my grandfather fought with Nelson at Trafalgar, and my father was an Englishman too, and my mother was an Englishwoman ; that so far as I can trace my descent back and back— and that is just as far as my grandfather—we are all English, every one of us. Well, there is not a day when I stand on the lake shore that I do not see the moors that were lifted up about my old habitation, and a little stone cottage nestling in among the greenery, and the glancing waters, and the lift of the lark up into heaven until you cannot see him, and a hundred other things besides that belong to this blessed place of my birth and breeding."

After leaving school he went to work at a small factory in the village, till he was old enough to learn a trade, and at fourteen he was taken as an apprentice by the Ilkley blacksmith, "John Birch," or "owd Jackie Birch," as he was generally styled, "and a pretty serious time I had of it away from home," wrote Mr. Collyer, "with a man for my master who died of drink." But the example in his case was powerless to harm. As showing his indefatigable love for reading at this period, while blowing the bellows he had a book fixed on a level with his head, so that at every motion he could catch a sentence and transfix it in the memory between-whiles ; a fact also showing how, under somewhat difficult circumstances, intellectual labour could be combined with physical, and where and how the early strata of a vast acquaintance with literature were laid from which he is never happier than in his illustrative quotations. Not seeing here so fair a prospect for his future as it appeared to him existed in America, he determined to cross the Atlantic, and in May, 1850, at the age of 26, having married a wife one day, sailed on the next for New York. He obtained work at his trade in Pennsylvania, which he yet followed, we believe, for ten years, preaching the while on Sundays in the Methodist Church, with which he had become connected as a lay preacher before he left his own country.

After Mr. Collyer's alienation from Methodism there happened to be a vacancy at a mission church in Chicago, to which he was appointed at the earnest recommendation of Dr. Furness—between whom and Mr. Collyer there now existed a unity of religious belief—and right well were the prognostications of his friend realised, for from the moment he undertook the charge its growth was assured, and a magnificent church arose in due course of time to prove by its presence the success of his ministrations. This edifice was burned down in the disastrous fire of 1871, only a fortnight after Mr. Collyer's return home from Europe— where he had been passing a three months' holiday—and while in England preaching the annual sermon for the Unitarian Conference in London. On the Sunday following the fire he called together his scattered flock, and, on the ruins of their church, read to them the touching words—doubly touching in their appositeness—from Isaiah, "Our holy and our beautiful house is burned up with fire, and all our pleasant things are laid waste," and after that spoke cheering words of courage and support to help them to bear with Christianlike fortitude their great losses. And this consolation came from one who had lost nearly his all—church, house, and library. The last-named must have been a grievous affliction, as it contained a precious collection of books very dear to its possessor. But there was one thing left to Robert Collyer, and that an unquenchable energy and activity which roused and inspired all with whom he came in contact, and displayed themselves in a more substantial manner by bringing about a restoration of the old order of things—one result being the erection on the former site of a new church, handsomer and more commodious than the one destroyed. In 1880, Mr. Collyer accepted the pastorate of the Church of the Messiah in New York, where he now labours.

Of Mr. Collyer's style of writing and speaking we give the following specimen. It is a contribution to an American journal, in reply to a letter which had appeared in its columns. "S. F.," the writer of the letter, had paid a recent visit to Ilkley, in Yorkshire. He was not much impressed with it apparently, his whole account of it, with the exception of a conversation with the natives in a fruitless effort to find Robert Collyer's mother, being given in the following sentences :— "Ilkley is a small town, striving to make a watering-place sensation, but with indifferent success. It has a rock cropping out which it calls a crag. It has wells whose waters are pure and cool. One or two of its fashionable Cures are palatial in appearance and exceedingly well kept." Rather a snubbing this for Ilkley and its many admirers.

The want of appreciation on the part of "S. F." brought forth the following beautiful sketch of the *Olicana* of the Romans :—

Chicago, August 23, 1873.

I notice that my dear friend S. F., in his exquisite letter in your paper of to-day, has been barking up the wrong tree in asking after my mother at Ilkley. My mother never lived there, and seldom visited the place. I went there when I was fourteen, to learn my trade with the same man who had taught my father, but my folks then lived over the moor six miles north, in a little place called Blubber Houses (Blueberry Houses), in Fewston parish, where at that time there was a great factory in full blast, now empty and deserted. I left the place in '38, my family left in '39, and went to Leeds, where my father died in '44, and where my mother still lives in a beautiful old age, and I write this because I am jealous for her ; if she had lived at Ilkley, S.F. would have found men and women there who would have remembered her better than they remember her son. She came now and then for a day's visit ; that was all.

But if he had gone into that queer old house by Bolton Bridge close to Rupert's Field, the house which was five hundred years ago a bridge chapel, and where he may still read this inscription on a great oaken beam :—

> Thou that wendest on this way,
> One Ave Maria thou shalt say,

and had said to good Hannah Williams, "Do you know Robert Collyer's mother?" she would have answered, "Yes, indeed. Why, she comes here and stays with me a week at a time, and I knew Robert when he was a lad : my brother and Robert were 'prentice together." And then she would have got him a piece of oat-cake and cheese and a glass of innocent home-brewed beer, and told him all about it.

And brother F. must please not to make game of Ilkley any more. Ilkley is neither to be sneered nor sneezed at ; it is a very notable as well as a very bonnie place. I wish I could have been with him. Is he interested in the poor, old, dim thoughts of God which came to the oldest and rudest worshippers? He would have found the same signs graven on those crags they find in India, in Central America, and in Scandinavia, the blind, dumb Bible of a word that was lost when the Druids lighted their fires on Brandreth and Brimham.

Does he care for the gallant fight the Briton of the north made for perhaps two centuries against the Roman? Those little streams east and west of the church,with the river on the north, and the wild hill to the south,were the boundaries of a city, such as it was, where these Brigantes made their stand and fought their forlorn battle, where they were beaten at last but not conquered, for they came back and burned the place over the head of the Legionaries who were there to hold it, and sent the eagles flying back, so that Severus had to come at last from Rome to get Lupus out of the scrape and restore such order as was possible.

Does he care about our own faith? It is a strong conjecture, supported by some of the best antiquaries, that wherever in Yorkshire you find the three Runic or Saxon crosses, there Paulinus preached and baptised, about 625, when the Saxon renounced his old gods, and set the cross above the raven. The crosses were there in Camden's time, 300 years ago. In my time the men of the church-warden period had made two of them gate-posts and one a sun-dial. Thoughtful John Snowden, the present vicar, has set them up again in the churchyard, in the right place. Here, certainly, was a church and a minister in 1085, and I have a complete list of the ministers since 1242. That queer little structure is one of the Mother churches of the North.

Does he care for great names? When Henry VIII. wanted a subsidy, in 1523, to fight the French (and serve them right), John Longfellow gave fourpence. That is the remotest man we can find of the line that has given us our most honoured poet. The family, or a part of it, seems to have gone to Horsforth, a few miles south and east, and from there possibly it came here ; but in 1523, there was no Longfellow on the subsidy roll for Horsforth. Ilkley is no doubt the nest of the Longfellows.

If, again, he had gone into that gabled farm-house a mile from Ilkley, on his way to Bolton, and had said to the old servant, "Is't maister about? I want to him. I'se an owd friend o' Robert Collyer," John Ellis would have said, "I'se glad to see ye. Sit down, And he would have sat in the great parlour where the Hebers lived and got ready to give us the man who wrote " From Greenland's Icy Mountains." Old Joe Smith, who lived to a very great age, who was our parish clerk, and who got to be so curiously old at last that we had to retire him after he told us that Mr. Burton, who was to leave us, would on the next Sunday preach his *funeral* sermon,—Old Joe used to tell us how his mother used to tell what a good woman the last Lady Heber was to the poor, so that the "Psalm of Life" and the "Missionary Hymn" go to Ilkley to find the head-waters of streams which make glad the city of God.

And does he bless anything which blesses our poor, broken bodies? That clear, gushing stream on the hill has healed the hearts of tens of thousands. There is a letter from Dr. Richardson, of Bierley, in Hearne's edition of Leland,

1712, in which the writer says that the well at Ilkley is a great resort for persons afflicted with scrofulas, and other like disorders. They found very great benefit from the waters, I suppose. I saw thousands from the great hives of industry to the south in my own day who were restored to health and strength at the old wells, and they have been doing this blessed work for two hundred years, I suppose. And then, last of all, if I could have gone with brother F. up to the moors, now all' abloom with the purple heather, and shown him little nooks I know of, where the brown waters tumble, and the rare ferns and mosses grow among the crags, and out on the great table-lands, where the shimmering sunshine these summer days seems to cover all things with a tremulous, translucent light, "clear as crystal like unto transparent glass," where there is a goodly smell of wild things I never caught here except on Nantucket; and if I could have sat with him in the stillness of a Sabbath morning, while the far-away music of the bells of Haworth floated up to meet the music of the bells of Ilkley, while the lark sang in the lift and the moor-birds answered from the coverts; and if I could have pointed out the old fastnesses of the Fairfaxes, the Cliffords, the Nortons and the Claphams; and told him a score of old legends he may never hear else, from the woe of Lady Rommelie, who lost her one child and founded the abbey, to the queer story of Mother Oddie, who saved one oat cake from the hungry Scots' raiders, in the '45, the only cake saved in all the town,—what a wonderful letter my good friend and your peerless correspondent could have written about my lovely old town, indeed.

Yours,

R. COLLYER.

Mr. Collyer has published three volumes of sermons, "Nature and Life" and "The Life that Now Is," which have run through numerous editions, and recently a small volume, "The Simple Truth," containing sermons or addresses, with texts chosen from the poets. His style is simple, clear, and nervous, carrying the reader along enwrapt by the rythmic flow of eloquent language which makes the sermons delightful reading. Possessed of a vivid imagination and a keen insight into the beauties of nature, which he describes with all the skill of a born poet ; and possessed also of an unbounded love for the solidarity of the human race which he has during the whole of his life striven to forward ; also possessed of an extensive acquaintance of men and things, studied through various phases, which he can portray in a highly realistic manner ; gifted with genuine humour, lighting up in a happy way the amusing side of human nature, and also with the power of describing the sorrowful and struggling side with a pathos that fills the heart with tender pity—these gifts are combined in the man who is rightly styled the "Poet Preacher of America."

Morley, near Leeds. THE EDITOR.

JOHN NICHOLSON

THE following incidents connected with the life of John Nicholson, the Airedale poet, will be read with interest by the many admirers of his writings. Spending an evening with a friend at Carlinghow, Batley, his host, while some of the family were engaged playing and singing the beautiful anthem "Hear my prayer," informed Nicholson of the recent decease of Mr. Wilkinson, of Carlinghow Hall, a gentleman of great literary taste and poetical turn of mind, when he immediately asked for pen and paper, and in a few minutes handed to his friend the following lines :—

> Dear Wilkinson is far above,
> Drinking the draughts of heavenly love,
> While I am in a world of care,
> Listening to "Hear my prayer."
> His prayer is heard.   The harp of Heaven
> Unto another bard is given.
> My friend has joined the choir of Heaven.

The following selections, showing Nicholson's skill in impromptu verse-making, are from the " Annals of Yorkshire " :—He was once on

John Nicholson.

the eve of having his furniture sold by Clarkson, his landlord, for rent, when his friend Mr. Fox prevented the sale by discharging the debt. He wrote on a pane of glass on one of the windows—

> Oh, Clarkson, Clarkson, with a heart
> More hard than Bingley rocks,
> Who would have sold the poet up
> But for his friend Lane Fox.

J. G. Horsfall one day called at the poet's house for a drink of water, when he was handed instead a draught of beer. Mr. Horsfall, in a jocose manner, said, "Nicholson, they state you are a poet, but let me hear what you can say about this pot of beer," when without premeditation he improvised the following :—

> O, for an everlasting spring
> Of home-brew'd drink like this !
> Then with my friends I'd laugh and sing
> And spend the hours in bliss ;
> Then come old Care, linked with Despair,
> For I, with thee made strong,
> Would plunge them overhead in beer,
> And make them lead the song.

A glass of newly-drawn porter was once brought to the poet, when he took out his pencil and wrote—

> The gallant, the gay, and the sporter,
> Have here but little to stay,
> For life's like the froth on that porter,
> And quickly doth vanish away.

The same authority says Nicholson was first brought into local reputation as a poet in 1818, by a sarcastic composition relating to a physician at Bradford. He afterwards wrote a piece in three acts, termed "The Robber of the Alps," which was performed at the Old Theatre, Bradford. It was so well received that he soon produced the "Siege of Bradford," which was acted for the benefit of Mr. Macaulay, one of the players, and yielded the sum of £47. In 1824 he published "Airedale" and other poems. A second edition was struck off in 1825. Unfortunately, the publication of this work induced him to quit his employment, and roam about the country for the purpose of selling the work. He then contracted inveterate habits of intemperance, which he never afterwards shook off, but instead they proved the bane and curse of his life. In 1827 he published the "Lyre of Ebor" and other poems, and again started as a vendor of his works. His improvident conduct continued to increase, and his wife and family had in consequence to endure many privations. The poet was often befriended and helped out of his difficulties by George Lane Fox, of Bramham. Believing that the metropolis was the great mart for his works, he visited London, accompanied by his wife, who proved a great check on his excesses. While there he buried a favourite child. A circumstance now occurred which put an end to his book-selling journeys. The printer and publisher of his works became insolvent, and a large stock of the books (Nicholson having paid for the paper) were put to the hammer, and realised about half their value. He was then obliged to earn a livelihood by the laborious and ill-recompensed occupation of wool-combing. He removed from Bingley to Bradford in 1833, and remained there during the remainder of his life, which was henceforward a chequered scene of labour one day and reckless conduct the next. He never gave up the pleasures of composing poetry,

H. Adlard Sc.

John Reed Appleton

F.S.A. LOND. & SCOT. &c.

and at intervals wrote " A description of the Lowmoor Ironworks," " A walk from Knaresborough to Harrogate," &c.   On the evening of Good Friday, April 13th, 1843, Nicholson left Bradford for Eldwick, and called at several places on the road.   It was near midnight when he left Shipley.   He proceeded up the bank of the canal in the direction of Dixon Mill, and at this place it seems attempted to cross the river Aire by means of the stepping stones.   The night was dark and the river swollen.   It is supposed that he had missed his footing and fallen into the current ; struggled out, became benumbed and exhausted.   He was found dead on the bank next morning, his body quite warm, and his clothes wet.   On the 18th he was interred in Bingley Churchyard.

Batley.   J. T.

JOHN REED APPLETON

JOHN REED APPLETON was born at Stockton-on-Tees, and cannot therefore be called a Yorkshireman, but, in many respects, he has a claim to a place in any " notes " relating to " Yorkshire Poets and Poetry."   He has sung in praise of our Yorkshire hills and dales, and his sympathies have ever been with its inhabitants.   Of our county he says :—

> Thy hills appear
> Again as olden friends,—rouse latent thought,
> Touching some sleeping chord of by-gone days,
> Of pleasant youthful memories, when, as now,
> The affluence of thy beauty lured my steps,
> Loving thee dearly for thy loveliness !

Mr. Appleton is descended from a family who held large possessions on the banks of the Tees, and his father, a man of ability and an excellent classical scholar, was a printer and publisher, and noted for his furtherance of local literature.   The subject of our sketch, though destined for the law, preferred the more congenial occupation of

commercial traveller, and in the intervals of business devoted himself to his favourite studies of poetry, painting, and music.   One study, that useful and pleasing science Archæology, has ever found in Mr. Appleton a constant and persevering disciple, though, in this, as in other branches of antiquarian knowledge, he has been more anxious to furnish other writers with interesting and trustworthy materials than to figure as an author himself.   He may be described as a painstaking student, and a careful and accurate writer on
Arms of Appleton.*   genealogical and heraldic subjects.   But it is as a poet, and as a Yorkshire poet, that we welcome

*The Arms of Appleton are:—Argent, a fesse sable between three apples in hanging position, stalked and leaved vert.   *Crest,* an Elephant's head couped, sable, tusked argent trunked or.

him to a place in "Old Yorkshire." Though not a prolific writer, his productions are characterized by the genius of true poetry, shewing that he has not only a close acquaintance with nature, but a keen perception of the beautiful. We have not space for long extracts, but give one specimen of his muse, from his poem on "Cleveland," a charming piece of word-painting.

> Lo ! ROSEBERRY—with stately head erect,
> Gorgeously gilded by the setting sun,
> In solemn silence on his misty throne
> Sits, towering over all—the landscape's King !
> While the bright clouds, as courtiers, stoop and kiss
> His emerald robe.

> In far, far other moods,
> I've seen him frown when heavy clouds have lain
> Upon his breast, and vivid lightnings gleamed,
> And from afar the muttering thunder roll'd,
> And wildest storm flew crashing through the dark
> Lone woods, and o'er the mountains' dreary paths ;
> While down the rocky slopes tumultuous poured
> Swoll'n cataracts with angry sullen roar !
> Anon—the veiling mist o'ercrept the dell,
> The sun burst radiant forth, and, instant, shewed
> Visions resplendent to the ravished eye !
> Scenes all-enchanting to the raptured sense !
> Defiant of the storm, more grandly sat
> The solemn mountain,—preaching still of God !

> And I have seen old Winter, with stern hand,
> Bind giant-icicles around his brow,
> And mantle him in frost, and load with snow
> The woods, and the bright babbling brooks congeal.
> Next have I watch'd young Spring, with fragrant breath
> Fold up, for Summer, Winter's frosty cloak,
> Dropping sweet flowers and blossoms as she went,
> And, with her roseate fingers, from the woods,
> Plucking the robes of snow ; and from ice-fetters
> Freeing the crystal streams, again to gush away !

Mr. Appleton is a Fellow of the Society of Antiquaries of London, Edinburgh, Newcastle-on-Tyne, and Copenhagen ; as well as a member of several other kindred societies : —

The earliest evidence for the Arms of Appleton are noticed in the " Herald and Genealogist " in the following terms :—

"This Seal presents on a shield of arms a chevron (diapered with the lines now used to designate gules) between three apples in a hanging position. It is not easy to make out the four objects which occupy the circular panels of the seal ; but the fourth is clearly a Katharine-wheel, and all were not improbably emblems of the saints to whom the clerk was devoted.
It may fairly be presumed that the Appletons scattered up and down on the Tees, arose from Appleton Wiske, in Allertonsnire or East Appleton, near Richmond. From the superior execution of the seal engraved, we are inclined to

SIGILLVM · WILL'I . DE · APPELTON · CL'ICI.

think that William de Appleton, like Wycliffe, was not merely named after the place of his birth, that his surname and arms were settled in his family, and that he belonged to a race of the name which occurs in considerable social status in the early part of the thirteenth century, in connection with the constables of Richmond.

The document, in the treasury of the Dean and Chapter of Durham, to which the seal is attached, does not contain any mention of its original owner. It is dated at Stockton (upon Tees) on Thursday after the Feast of the Purification of B. V. M., 1370, and is a quitclaim by Robert Lukline, chaplain, to William Chapman, of " Wlston, " (*hodie* Wolviston) of the grantor's right in all the lands which the same Chapman and he had in " Wlliston," of the gift of Thomas de Gretham. It does not follow conclusively that Appleton was then dead ; but as he is not a witness, and the instrument does not state that his seal was borrowed in consequence of the grantor's not being known, the probability is that he was so, and that is was appropriated by Robert Lukline to his own use."

Morley, near Leeds.　　　　　　　　　　　THE EDITOR.

ROBERT BASTON

ROBERT BASTON was born in Yorkshire, somewhere on the borders of Nottinghamshire, about the middle of the thirteenth century, and died in 1310. He was educated at the Carmelite School or College, Oxford, where " he deservedly carried away the bays in poetry and rhetoric," and became Public Orator of the University. On leaving Oxford he entered the Carmelite Friary at Scarborough, and eventually became head of the house King Edward I., on his expedition to Scotland in 1304, took Baston with him to sing his victories in heroic verses, who produced a poem in celebration of the siege of Stirling. The following year he was again in Scotland, when he was taken prisoner, and was, " by the overpowering commands and severities of Robert Bruce, obliged to recant all, and to extol the Scotch nation as highly as he had lately magnified the English," the price of his ransom being a poem on Bruce, in the same style as that of the " Siege of Stirling." He therefore set to work and produced " A Panegyric on Robert Bruce," and was set at liberty. The poem was published in " Fordun's Scotæ Chronicon," Oxford, 1722. He wrote chiefly in Latin, several of his works being still extant, and a few poems in English, none of which have come down. Yorkshire may also claim some sort of connection with two other Laureates—Dr. Thomas Warton, 1785-1790, and William Wordsworth, 1843-1850 ; both of whom were descended from old Yorkshire families.

London.　　　　　　　　　　　F. ROSS.

CHARLES WILLIAM SIKES

IR CHARLES W. SIKES, Managing Director of the Huddersfield Banking Company, on whom Her Majesty has recently conferred the honour of knighthood, in recognition of the important part taken by him in introducing the system of Post Office Savings Banks, is the second son of the late Mr. Shakespear Garrick Sikes, banker, of Huddersfield, who died in 1862. His mother was Hannah, daughter of Mr. John Hirst, also of Huddersfield; and he was born in the year 1818. When at school, he received, as a prize, a copy of Dr. Franklin's " Essays and Letters," which he read with great interest. This book implanted in his mind the germs of many useful thoughts, and exercised a powerful influence in giving a practical turn to his life. Having seen a number of men begging when out of work, young Sikes wondered whether they had ever heard of Dr. Franklin and of his method of avoiding beggary or bad times by saving their money when trade was brisk and they were well paid.

In 1833 Mr. Sikes entered the service of the Huddersfield Banking Company, which was the second joint stock bank that had been established in England. The prudence and success with which Scotch banking companies had been conducted induced the directors to select a Scotch manager; and one of the first resolutions the directors adopted was to give deposit receipts for sums of ten pounds and upwards, for the purpose of encouraging the working classes in habits of providence and thrift. Mr. Sikes, being somewhat of a favourite with the manager, often heard from his lips most interesting accounts of the provident habits of the Scotch peasantry, and was informed by him of the fact that one of the banks at Perth paid not less than twenty thousand pounds a year, as interest on deposits, varying from ten to two hundred pounds each. In 1837, Mr. Sikes became one of the cashiers of the Huddersfield Banking Company. This brought him into direct contact and intercourse with the very class which, from the direction his mind was taking, he so much wished to understand—namely, the thrifty portion of the industrious classes. A considerable number of them had sums lying at interest. As years rolled on Mr. Sikes often witnessed the depositor commencing with ten or twenty pounds; then, by degrees, making permanent additions to his little store, until at length the amount would reach one, two, or, in some few instances, even three hundred pounds. Mr. Sikes would often imagine the marvellous improvement that would be effected on the condition of the working classes, if every one of them became influenced by the same frugality and forethought which induced these exceptional operatives to deposit their savings at his bank. Mr Sikes was convinced that national prosperity, as well as national adversity, might be attended with great evils, unless the masses were endowed with habits of providence and thrift, and prepared, by previous education, for the " good time coming."

Many discussions with working men, in his homeward evening walks, convinced Mr. Sikes that there were social problems, with which legislation would be almost powerless to grapple, and of these the thriftlessness of the masses of the people was one. An employer of five hundred hand-loom weavers had told Mr. Sikes that, in a previous period of prosperity, when work was abundant and wages were very high, he could not, had he begged on bended knee, have induced his men to save a single penny, or to lay by anything for a rainy day.

It was at this period that Mr. Sikes was reading the late Archbishop Sumner's " Records of Creation," and met with the following passage :—" The only true secret of assisting the poor, is to make them agents in bettering their own condition." Simple as are the words, they shed light into Mr. Sikes' mind, and became the key-note and the test to which he brought the various views and theories which he had previously met with—doles and charities, though founded frequently on the most benevolent motives, were too often deteriorating to their recipients. On the other hand, if self-reliance and self-help could only be made characteristics of the working classes generally, nothing could retard their onward and upward progress. Mr. Sikes observed, that, until the working-classes had more of the money power in their hands, they would still be periodically in poverty and distress. He saw that if provident habits could only be generally pursued by them, the face of society would immediately be transformed ; and he resolved, in so far as lay in his power, to give every aid to this good work. From his own reading and observation, stimulated by what he had learnt as to the facilities offered in Scotland for the cultivation of habits of providence, Mr. Sikes became impressed with the necessity of extending and multiplying the then existing Savings Banks, so as to bring them into closer connection with the daily life and requirements of the people

In 1850, Savings Banks were only open a very few hours in each week. In Huddersfield, where more than £400,000 a year was paid in wages, the Savings Bank, after having been established over thirty years, had only accumulated £74,332. In the same year, Mr. Sikes addressed an anonymous letter to the editors of the *Leeds Mercury*, to which, by their request, he afterwards attached his name. In that letter he recommended the formation of Penny Savings Banks in connection with mechanics' institutes, mills, workshops, and schools. In simple words, but with many telling facts, he showed how the young men and the young women of the working-classes were growing up deprived of almost every opportunity of forming habits of thrift, and of becoming depositors in Savings Banks. The letter was received with general approbation. The committee of the Yorkshire Union of Mechanics' Institutes gave their cordial sanction to it ; and Penny Banks were established in connection with nearly every Mechanics' Institute in Yorkshire. Mr. Sikes personally commenced one at Huddersfield ; and down to the present time it has received and repaid about £30,000. In fact, the working people of Huddersfield, doubtless owing, in some measure, to the practical counsel of Mr. Sikes, have become most provident and thrifty ; the deposits in their Savings Bank having increased from £74,000 in 1850, to £383,000 in 1880.

In 1854, Mr. Sikes published his excellent pamphlet on " Good Times ; or the Savings Bank and the Fireside," and the success which it met with—indicated by a sale of over 40,000 copies—induced him to give his attention to the subject of Savings Banks generally. He was surprised to find that they were so utterly inadequate to meet the requirements of the country. He sought an interview with Sir George Cornewall Lewis, then Chancellor of the Exchequer, and brought the subject under his consideration. The Chancellor requested Mr. Sikes to embody his views in a letter, and in the course of a few months there appeared a pamphlet, addressed to Sir Cornewall Lewis, entitled, "Savings Banks Reform." Mr. Sikes wished to insist on the Government guarantee being given for deposits made in Savings Banks, but this was refused. He next proceeded to ventilate the question of Post Office Savings Banks, being disappointed that no measure for the improvement of Savings Banks in general had been adopted by Parliament. The day appeared very distant when his cherished wish would be realised—that the Savings Bank would really become the bank of the people. But the darkest hour precedes the dawn. When he had almost given up the notion of improving the existing Savings Banks, the idea suddenly struck him that in the Money Order Office there was the very organisation which might be made the basis of a popular Savings Bank. Mr. Sikes communicated his plan in a letter to his friend, Mr. (now Sir Edward) Baines ; then member for Leeds, whose life-long services to the best interests of the working classes are so widely known. The plan was submitted to Sir Rowland Hill, who approved of the suggestion, and considered the scheme " practicable, as far as the Post Office was concerned." In the recent "Life of Sir Rowland Hill, K.C.B.," the following just and highly complimentary tribute has been paid to Mr. C. W. Sikes, as the originator of the Post Office Savings Bank system :—

"In the year 1859 the first move was made towards that important "improvement, the establishment of the Post Office Savings Bank; "Mr. Edward Baines, M.P., for Leeds, enclosing to me unofficially, but "with a request for attention, a paper on the subject, drawn up by "Mr. Charles William Sikes, of Huddersfield, the originator of the "plan. I wrote on August 2nd, to express my concurrence in Mr. "Sikes's views, and my readiness to do what I could towards giving "them effect. My letter was as follows :—

August 2nd, 1859.

"My dear Sir,—Pray excuse the unavoidable delay in replying to your letter "of the 30th ult.

"With modifications which could readily be introduced, Mr. Sikes's plan is, "in my opinion, practicable so far as the Post Office is concerned.

"The plan also appears to me to be practicable in its other parts; but on "these I would suggest the expediency of taking the opinion of some one "thoroughly conversant with ordinary banking business, and who is acquainted "also with savings banks.

"I need not add that, if carried into effect, the plan would, in my opinion, "prove highly useful to the public, and in some degree advantageous to the revenue.

"I shall be most happy, when the time arrives for so doing, to submit it for "the approval of the Postmaster-General.—Faithfully yours,

"ROWLAND HILL.

"E. Baines, Esq., M.P., Reform Club."

"Mr. Sikes, I must not omit to say, never received nor ever sought "any advantage, pecuniary or otherwise, in recompense for his admirable "suggestion, contenting himself with the deep gratification of having "done what lay in his power to confer an inestimable benefit on the "humbler classes of his countrymen.

"Mr. Gladstone, then Chancellor of the Exchequer, at once took "up the scheme warmly, and subsequently carried the measure through "Parliament, the machinery for giving it effect being devised by "Messrs. Scudamore and Chetwynd."

Mr. Gladstone, in 1861, carried the Bill through Parliament, for the establishment of Post Office Savings Banks throughout the country. Mr. Sikes, when predicting, at the Social Science Association, the success of the Post Office Savings Banks, spoke in the following words:— "Should the plan be carried out, it will soon be doing a glorious work. Wherever a bank is opened and deposits received, self-reliance will to some extent be aroused, and with many, a nobler life will be begun. They will gradually discern how ruthless an enemy is improvidence to working men ; and how truly his friends are economy and forethought. Under their guidance, household purchases could be made on the most favoured terms for cash ; any wished-for house taken at the lowest rent for punctual payment ; and the home enriched with comforts, until it is enjoyed and prized by all. From such firesides go forth those inheriting the right spirit—loving industry, loving thrift, and loving home. Emulous of a good example, they, in their day and generation, would nobly endeavour to lay by a portion of their income. Many a hard winter and many a slack time would be comfortably got over by drawing on the little fund, to be again replenished in better days. And if the plan were adopted, remembering that it would virtually bring the Savings Bank within less than an hour's walk of the fireside of every working man in the United Kingdom, I trust that it is not taking too sanguine a view to anticipate that it would render aid in ultimately winning over the rank and file of the industrial classes of the kingdom, to those habits of forethought and self-denial, which bring enduring reward to the individual, and materially add to the safety of the State." The working classes have not yet, however, taken full advantage of the facilities in saving afforded them by the Post Office Savings Banks ; the institution being still too young to have fully taken root. We believe that the living generation must pass away before the full fruits of the Post Office Savings Banks can be gathered in ; and that Sir Charles William Sikes' name will ever hold a distinguished place in connection with those valuable institutions.

The results of the Post Office Savings Banks Act have so far proved entirely satisfactory ; and the Money Order Offices have been largely extended. They are now over 6,000 in number, consequently the facilities in saving have been multiplied ten-fold since the banks were established, there being only 597 Savings Banks in 1859 in the United Kingdom. The number in the London district is now about 560, so that from any point in the thickly populated parts of the Metropolis a Savings Bank may be found within a distance of a few hundred yards. The number of the depositors at the end of 1880 reached 2,185,000, while the amount of deposits amounted to £33,744,637 sterling. At the same time the amount deposited with the original Savings Banks remained about the same.

It appears from the 26th report of the Postmaster-General, issued on the 14th August, 1880, that from September, 1861, to 31st December, 1879, the number of Post Office Savings Banks opened was 6,016. Within the same interval there have been 40,250,430 deposits, amounting (including interest) to £121,643,088, and the total amount repaid to depositors has been £89,630,954, leaving the amount still deposited £32,012,134, belonging to 1,988,477 depositors. The total amount of deposits, with the interest due, had on the 31st of December 1880, reached £33,744,637, showing an increase of £1,732,503 over the amount recorded on the corresponding day of 1879. Whilst the management of the old Trustees Savings Banks has resulted in a heavy loss to the country, the amount of net profits of the Post Office Savings Banks to 31st December, 1879—after paying all expenses, and £97,084 on account of the new building in Queen Victoria Street in addition— has been £1,131,000. The importance and full significance of these enormous totals, as indicative of the genuine progress and increased social well-being of our people cannot easily be over-estimated. Therefore, early this year, a memorial was sent to the Premier from the mayor and leading inhabitants of Huddersfield suggesting that some public acknowledgment should be made of their townsman's highly-deserving services. Before this memorial reached Mr. Gladstone, that right honourable gentleman had already written to Mr. Sikes, informing him of Her Majesty's intention to confer a knighthood upon him. This was hailed with pleasure, not only in financial and commercial circles, but also by Sir Charles Sikes' numerous friends in Yorkshire, and by others of his countrymen who rejoice to see public services fitly recognised.

The class of private bankers have furnished many illustrious recruits to the nobility and titled gentry ; but Sir Charles William Sikes is the first and only Joint Stock bank manager who has received the honour of knighthood. We are not surprised to learn that the shareholders of the bank have already altered its constitution, to allow Sir Charles being appointed the managing director. The new knight is not only a banker of high repute for ability, shrewdness, and spotless integrity, but is also a gentleman of large information and culture, having taken from youth upwards a keen delight in the works of great authors.

It has been proposed in Huddersfield to have a portrait of this public benefactor placed in one of the public institutions of that town, and also to raise a sum of £3,000 for the endowment of local scholarships or prizes, in honour of Sir Charles Sikes, and in association with his name for the encouragement of deserving students.

Though somewhat tardy, Sir Charles Sikes's reward has come at last, and that from a statesman of great repute as a financier, and one, moreover, to whom party spirit has never imputed selfishness and indiscrimination in his distribution of honours. We may further express the hope that Sir Charles William Sikes will long live to enjoy his knighthood. The honour, we feel convinced, is nothing in his estimation compared with the gratification of knowing that he has been of great service to his country, by employing the talents with which he is endowed, and which his own industry improved, in benefiting the pockets, and therefore promoting the happiness, not only of thousands unknown to himself, but of millions yet unborn.

Abridged from the BIOGRAPH.

RICHARD THORNTON

RICHARD THORNTON was born at Cottingley, near Bingley ; and the writer of this can well remember seeing him, when a boy attending school, ride into Bradford on a pony or donkey. As he grew up, he showed such an aptitude for studies of a scientific kind that his family, who had removed to Horton Road, Bradford, decided to send him to the School of Mines, in London; and when the great traveller, Dr. David Livingstone, proposed to revisit Africa in the year 1858, Sir R. I. Murchison recommended young Thornton to him, as an excellent geologist and geographer. Accordingly, in March, 1858, he left our shores with this prince of explorers, and after spending some time on the Zambesi, he detached himself from the party, and accompanied the great German traveller, the Baron C. von der Decken, in his first survey of the Kilimandjaro Mountains. These mountains, although in Africa, are covered on their tops or peaks with eternal snows. Here young Thornton drew the first contoured map of that wild and lofty country, took many observations of latitude and longitude, and kept an accurate diary. Copies of all these writings, as well as his original map, have been sent by his family to the Royal Geographical Society.

On the 23rd of May, 1864, the Founder's gold medal of the Royal Geographical Society was presented to Baron C. von der Decken, for his two surveys of Kilimandjaro, which he ascertained to have an altitude of 20,065 feet. In returning thanks he spoke as follows: "Happy and proud as I am to-day, there is still some sadness mingled with it. I miss here my poor friend, the late Mr. Richard Thornton, your countryman, and my companion during my first excursion to Kilimandjaro. We did not at that time reach so great an elevation as I did in my second journey, in which, with the aid of Dr. Karsten, I corrected the mistakes of the first. Thornton was, nevertheless, the first European besides myself who penetrated further than the low hills surrounding the great mountain, and settled by his testimony the question of snowy mountains in equatorial Africa. He was a good companion, and extremely useful during the expedition by taking observations, working very laboriously with the theodolite, and as a geologist in collecting and describing the rocks. If I ever come back to Europe and publish an account of my travels, I shall not omit to give due credit to my lamented companion.

On the same occasion, being the annual meeting of the society, Sir Roderick Impey Murchison, its distinguished president, spoke of him thus, and a more graceful compliment could not be imagined. He said (after giving some notices of others who had died during the year):

I have now to speak of a gifted and promising young man, Mr. Richard Thornton, of Bradford, who has lost his life by his zealous exertions to extend our acquaintance with the geography and geology of Eastern Africa. I am proud to say that Richard Thornton received his scientific education in the Royal School of Mines, over which I preside, and that, being desirous of accompanying Livingstone in his last explorations, I confidently recommended him to the good will of the great traveller. When Livingstone last left our shores in March, 1858, young Thornton, then only nineteen years of age, accompanied him as geologist. Qualifying himself during the voyage, and at the Cape of Good Hope, in making astronomical calculations, and being also a good sketcher of ground and capable of constructing maps, he was as well adapted to lay down the physical geography of the Zambesi river as to describe the various rocks which occupy its banks. In looking over his accurately-kept diaries, in which he never failed to register every fact, I find that he made upwards of 7,000 observations, to fix relative geographical points, and to determine altitudes on the banks of the Zambesi. In leaving the tertiary rocks of the Delta behind him, and in ascending that river to the rapids, he described numerous rocks of igneous origin; and, still further inland, various seams of thick and good coal (of which the Portuguese may very largely avail themselves); proving by the associated fossil remains, that the coal was of the old and best age of that mineral. His health having failed, he was for awhile estranged from the Zambesi expedition, through a partial misunderstanding between his chief and himself. This having been completely done away with when my young friend returned to work out and complete his labours in the Zambesi region, I should not here have alluded to it, if not to recount the important services he rendered in the meantime to geographical and geological science, by becoming *ad interim* the scientific companion of Baron C. von der Decken, in his first survey of the Kilimandjaro Mountains, from Zanzibar and Mombas. Having recently examined the diary kept by Mr. Richard Thornton in that journey between Mombas and the highest point the travellers reached, and also on their return to Mombas, or between the last days of June and the 10th of October, I have no hesitation in saying that the labour is so geograpically detailed, every movement so accurately recorded, the transactions with the various native tribes so clearly explained, and every hour of the 120 days' expedition so well accounted for, that, with the contoured map of the region which he prepared, together with many sketches of the form of the ground, I can really fancy myself, like his leader and himself, struggling to reach the snowy equatorial summits. The numerous obstacles opposed by the native chiefs, and the manner in which, after so many " showrys " or palavers, all difficulties were overcome ; the perfect description of the habits and dresses of the natives—of the metamorphosed structure of the rocks— the vegetation of each zone of altitude—all these are given ; whilst every moment of clear weather in that humid region was devoted to star and lunar observations, or to theodolite measurements of altitude, and the fixing of relative geographical points. All this, too, was scrupulously performed by Thornton, notwithstanding occasional attacks of fever, to which the Baron and himself were subjected. I cannot but hope that these diaries of an accurately minute philosopher, or at least large portions of them, will appear in print ; for I have read few writings more instructive and characteristic. In fact, until Baron von der Decken and Thornton carried out this expedition, no other African traveller has ever had presented to him such a vast variety of scenes of nature, within so limited a compass, as those which are seen in ascending from the eastern seaboard to the banana-groves on the skirts of the snow-clad peaks of Kilimandjaro. As the account of this first ascent has been given to Continental Europe in German, so we may rejoice that our Thornton's English version of the same may soon appear; whilst Baron von der Decken, our Medallist of this year, unites with me in the expression of admiration of the undaunted efforts and able assistance of his companion. In truth, in his letters to myself, besides what is noted down in his diaries, Thornton correctly described (and for the first time) the nature of each rock in that region; by which I clearly learned that igneous rocks, whether syenites or porphyries, had penetrated micaceous slaty metamorphic strata, and that streams of vesicular lava, which occur on the flanks of the mountains, indicated clearly that the loftiest summits, now capped with snow, had been raised by the extrusion of a great subaërial volcano. If his life had been spared, this fine young man intended, as he wrote to me, to endeavour to traverse Africa, and compare its East and West Coasts with each other, as well as with its vast lacustrine centre. Anxious, however, to finish off in the meantime those labours on the Zambesi which he had so far advanced, he rejoined his old chief, Livingstone, and was on the point of completing a map of a mountainous tract on the north bank of the stream, when, in over-exerting himself, he fell a victim to that fever which has proved so fatal to our missionaries, to the devoted wife of Livingstone, and which, on more than one occasion, has nearly deprived of life that great traveller himself. One of his companions for a time on the Zambesi, the Rev. Henry Rowley, in writing to me of the never-flagging zeal and unconquerable energy, as well as of the generous nature and high character of Richard Thornton, adds:—"Axe in hand, he would cut himself a path to the top of a thickly-wooded mountain, never leaving it till the setting sun made further observations impossible." In reviewing the journals and diaries of Richard Thornton, I am lost in admiration of his patient labours of registration, when combined with his vivacity of description. With such a delineator in words as Thornton, and such an artist as Mr. Baines—who has sent home such admirable coloured drawings of South-African scenes, particularly of the Falls of the Zambesi—those of us who are destined never to be able to penetrate into the southern part of Africa, may quite realise to our mind's eye the true character of that grand continent. Through the devotion of the brothers and sisters of the deceased traveller, the whole of his voluminous notes and observations have, I am happy to say, been carefully copied out and transmitted to us: and I am confident that every one who examines them will declare with myself, that Richard Thornton was so gifted and rising an explorer, that, had he lived, his indomitable zeal and his great acquirements would have surely placed him in the front rank of men of science. He died on the 21st April, 1863, at the early age of 25 years.

The following extract of a letter from Dr. Livingstone to Sir Roderick I. Murchison, contains a brief account of his last illness and death.

Murchison Cataracts (on the Shire), April 25.

My dear Sir Roderick,—With sorrow,I have to communicate the sad intelligence that Mr. Richard Thornton died on the 21st current. He performed a most fatiguing journey from this to Tette and back again, and that seemed to use up all his strength ; for, thereafter, he could make no exertion without painful exhaustion. His object was to connect his bearings of the hills at Tette (on the Zambesi) with the mountains here. I knew nothing of his resolution till after he had left. He had resolved to go home after he had examined Zomba and the Melanje range, but on the 11th he was troubled with diarrhœa, which ran on to dysentery and fever. We hoped to the last that his youth and unimpaired constitution would carry him through, as he had suffered comparatively little from fever; but we were disappointed. An insidious delirium prevented us learning aught of his last wishes. All his papers, &c., were at once sealed up, and are sent home to his brother at Bradford. He is buried about 500 yards from the foot of the first cataract, and on the right bank of the Shire. * * * ."

Eldwick.   ABRAHAM HOLROYD.

JOHN TRAVIS

JOHN TRAVIS, surgeon and naturalist, though not a native of Scarborough, the name of this justly distinguished individual is constantly associated with its history. He was born at Yarm, in this county, on the 7th February, 1724. He received a classical education at the Grammar School, Scorton, near Catterick, then under the management of the Rev. J. Noble, B.A. After he had finished his studies at Scorton, he came to Scarborough on a visit to his grand-father, Mr. Hugh Travis; here he was articled as a medical pupil to Mr. Culmer Cockerill, then the leading practitioner in the town. At the close of his apprenticeship he went to London, in order to perfect himself as far as possible in his professional pursuits. During his stay in town he obtained introductions to and formed an acquaintance with those eminent characters, John Hunter and Dr. Fothergill, and continued in correspondence and friendship with them as long as they lived. On his return to Scarborough he entered into partnership with Mr. Cockerill, and continued his practice with ardour and success. In 1757, when he was about thirty-three years of age, he published an essay, which discovers great purity of style, classical research, and scientific knowledge, tending to show that the use of copper vessels in the navy was one principal cause of sea scurvy. (*Vide* Medical Observations and Inquiries, vol. ii., pp. 1 and 90.) This essay attracted some attention, especially amongst several of the Fellows of the Royal Society, and led to the substitution of iron instead of copper boilers. The next year he published a paper on an accident then imperfectly understood, "The Luxation of the Thigh-bone." The essay is thought by competent judges to display extensive knowledge of the subject, and of the appropriate means of reduction. He was distinguished not only as a successful medical practitioner, but also as a naturalist and philosopher. The late Mr. Pennant, on his tour to

Scotland, did him the honour twice to visit him; and the pages of " British Zoology " not only show his accuracy, especially in icthyology, but the estimation in which he was held by this eminent writer. His account of the fishing grounds, and mode of fishing at Scarborough, inserted in the History of Scarborough, present a specimen of chaste and elegant composition. Nor was his sphere of usefulness confined to pursuits of this kind; he was four times called to fill the magisterial chair, and was for many years the father of the Corporation of Scarborough. His disposition was cheerful and communicative, and his well-stored mind rendered his society deeply interesting. Mr. Travis was twice married, and had four sons and six daughters. Through life he exhibited the practical influence of Christian principles, and died August 22nd, 1794, full of the hope of a blessed immortality. His epitaph on a tombstone in Scarborough churchyard, with the date of the year, written by himself, gives to a reflecting mind a striking admonition, and shows in the writer a calm resignation to the expected summons :—

JOHANNES TRAVIS.
Mortalis esse desut,
Anno Salutis, 1794. Dd. æt. 71.
Nascentes morimur, finisque ab origine pendet.
Reader ! Redeem the time,—repent,—amend !
Life hath no length,—Eternity no end.

Scarborough.   THE LATE T. WALLER.

NICHOLAS SAUNDERSON

MR. NICHOLAS SAUNDERSON, the Blind Professor of Mathematics at Cambridge, was born at Thurleston, in Yorkshire, in 1682, and when two years of age was deprived of sight by the smallpox. The history of this remarkable man is well worthy of preservation. His father's name was John. He was employed in the Excise. The blind boy is reported to have taught himself to read by tracing out the letters with his fingers on the gravestones in the churchyard of his parish. He was afterwards sent to the Grammar School at Penistone : then under the care of a Mr. Staniforth, but not being able to read himself, could only listen to others, yet he soon made considerable progress in classical learning. It is stated that Virgil and Horace were his favourites among the Roman writers, and he would quote them in conversation with great propriety and without any appearance of pedantry. But Euclid, Archimedes, and Diophantus, and some other mathematicians, were the authors he chiefly studied in the Greek language. He had been taught arithmetic by his father, and was soon able to make very long calculations by the strength of his memory, and to invent new rules for the solution of arithmetical problems, with great ease. Dr. Nettleton, of Halifax, taught him the principles of algebra and geometry.   He then went to an Academy at Attercliffe, near Sheffield, where he made himself master of logic and metaphysics.   At length, by the help of his friends, he went to Cambridge, to teach philosophy in that University.   He was not admitted into any college, but chose Christ's College for his residence. Here the celebrated Professor Whiston showed him much attention and rendered him great assistance ; and when Mr. Whiston was removed from the Lucasian Professorship of Mathematics, Saunderson was appointed to the vacant chair.   When George II. visited that University in 1728, Professor Saunderson was created Doctor of Laws by His Majesty's command.   He died April 19th, 1739, in the fifty-seventh year of his age.

Morley, near Leeds.   THE EDITOR.

JOHN DAWSON

JOHN DAWSON, a self-taught mathematician of the highest order, was born at Garsdale, in the parish of Sedbergh, in 1734, and was the son of poor parents.   In early life he used to tend sheep on the hills, and the stone is yet pointed out upon which he used to sit, solving the most abstruse mathematical problems mentally, without either the aid of book or slate, and he had received no education whatever beyond that which a village school could furnish in those days.   He was afterwards articled to a surgeon in Lancaster, and settled at Sedbergh, as a surgeon and mathematical teacher, where he died in 1820, aged 86 years.   There is a monument to him in the nave of the church at Sedbergh, placed between two of the arches, and above it his bust carved by Flaxman, the forehead indicating mental power of the highest order.   The following inscription is placed beneath it : —

IN MEMORY OF
JOHN DAWSON, OF SEDBERGH,
WHO DIED ON THE 19TH OF SEPTEMBER, 1820, AGED 86
YEARS.
DISTINGUISHED BY HIS PROFOUND KNOWLEDGE
OF MATHEMATICS,
BELOVED FOR HIS AMIABLE SIMPLICITY OF
CHARACTER,
AND REVERED FOR HIS EXEMPLARY DISCHARGE
OF EVERY HOME AND RELIGIOUS DUTY,
THIS MONUMENT WAS ERECTED BY HIS
GRATEFUL PUPILS, AS A LAST TRIBUTE OF
AFFECTION AND ESTEEM.

No less than eleven of his pupils were Senior Wranglers at Cambridge. In 1771, Starkie, of St. John's; 1781, Ainslie, of Pembroke; 1786,

Bell, Trinity, the eminent Chancery barrister, commonly called Jockie Bell ; 1789, Millers, St. John's ; 1792, Palmer, St. John's ; 1793, Harrison, Queen's ; 1794, Butler, Sidney Sussex, afterwards Head Master of Harrow and Dean of Peterborough ; 1797, Hudson, Trinity; 1798, Sowerby, Trinity ; 1800, Inman, St. John's ; 1807, Gipps, St John's. In 1808, Bland, of St. John's, another pupil, was Second Wrangler ; and a third, perhaps the most celebrated of all in his after career, was fifth on the list, Adam Sedgwick. There is a fine folio engraving in existence, representing Dawson in a standing posture, and pointing with his finger to an open book, over which a pupil, with his back to the spectator, is bending, concerning whose identity many theories have been raised. The engraving was published in 1809, by Colnaghi, of Cockspur Street, London.

ABRAHAM SHARP

Mr. ABRAHAM SHARP, an eminent mathematician and mechanic, was descended from an ancient family, and was a relative of Archbishop Sharp, of Little Horton, Bradford, in the West Riding of Yorkshire. At a proper age he was put apprentice to a merchant in Manchester, but his genius and disposition became so remarkable for the study of mathematics, not only in the practical, but also in the speculative parts, that he soon became uneasy in that situation of life, and by the mutual consent of his master and himself, though not of his father, he quitted the employ of the merchant and removed to Liverpool, where, according to his natural bent, he gave himself up wholly to the study of mathematics and astronomy. He opened a school and taught writing, accounts, &c. He did not long continue in Liverpool before he accidentally fell in company with a London merchant or tradesman, under whose roof the famous astrologer, Mr. Flamsteed, lived ; and that he might be personally with that eminent man, when he left Liverpool he engaged with the merchant in the capacity of a book-keeper. It was here that he first contracted an intimate friendship with Mr. Flamsteed, by whose interest and recommendation he attained a more lucrative employ than a bookkeeper in the Dockyard at Chatham, where he continued till his friend and patron, knowing his great merit and abilities, called him to his assistance in fitting up the astronomical apparatus in the Royal Observatory at Greenwich, now called Flamsteed House, which had been built about the year 1676, Mr. Flamsteed being about that time thirty years of age, and Mr. Sharp twenty-five. In this situation he continued to assist Mr. Flamsteed in making observations on the mural arch of nearly seven feet radius, and 140 degrees on the limb of the meridianal zenith ; distances of the fixed stars, sun, moon, and the other planets, with the time of their transits over the meridian ; together with observations of the sun and moon, of Jupiter's satellites, variations of the compass, &c. He likewise assisted him in taking a catalogue of the right ascensions and distances from the poles, longitude and magnitudes of 3,000 fixed stars, while they change the longitudes one degree. But, from a continual observance of the stars at night in a cold, thin air, joined to a weakly constitution, he was reduced to a bad state of health, for the recovery of which he desired leave to return to his home at Horton, where, as soon as he found himself recovering, he began to fit up an observatory of his own, having first made an elegant and curious engine for turning all kinds of work in wood or brass, with a mandrel for turning irregular figures, ovals, roses, wreathed pillars, &c. ; besides which he made most of. the tools used by joiners, clockmakers, opticians, and mathematical instrument makers. The limbs of his large equatorial instrument, sextant, quadrant, &c., graduated with the nicest accuracy by diagonal divisions, were all his own making. The telescopes he made use of were adjusted with his own hands, making the lenses ground figured. He assisted Mr. Flamsteed in calculating most of the tables in the second volume of his " Historia Celestis," as appears by their letters, now seen at Horton ; likewise the curious drawings of the charts of all constellations visible in our hemisphere ; together with the still more excellent drawings of the planispheres, both of the Northern and Southern constellations, which were sent to be engraved at Amsterdam by a masterly hand ; yet the originals far exceeded the engravings in point of beauty and elegance. These were published by Mr. Flamsteed. The mathematician meets with something extraordinary in his elaborate treatise of " Geometry Improved by a large and accurate table, exemplified in making logarithms on natural numbers from them to sixty places or figures," there being a table of them all—primes to 1,100, trine to 61 figures. Likewise his concise treatise of Poledra, or solid bodies ; twelve new ones, with various methods of forming them, and their exact dimensions and solids in numbers, illustrated with a variety of neatly engraved copper-plates by his own hands ; also the models of those Poledras he cut out in a most amazing and exact manner in boxwood. Few or none of the mathematical instrument makers could excel him in exactly graduating or engraving any mathematical or astronomical instrument--sextant, quadrants of various sorts, dials, armillary sphere ; besides the common properties, his moveable circles for exhibiting and solving all spherical triangles, &c., all contrived, graduated, and finished in an elegant manner by himself. In short, he had a remarkably clear head for executing anything, not only in mechanics, drawing, writing, and beautiful schemes of figures, but in all his calculations and geometrical constructions. The quadrature of the circle was undertaken by him for his own private amusement in the year 1699, deducted from two different series, whereby the truth thereof is proved by seventy-two figures. He also calculated the logarith metre, sines, and tangents of scants of the seconds to every minute of the first degree of the quadrant. These laborious investigations most probably may be seen at the Royal Society, as they were presented to the Rev. Patrick Murdock. He kept up a correspondence by letters with most of the eminent mathematicians and astronomers of his time—Mr. Flamsteed, Sir Isaac Newton, Dr. Halley, Dr. Wallis, Mr. Hodgson, Mr. Sherwin, &c. From a great variety of letters it is evident that Mr. Sharp spared neither pains nor time to promote real science. He was a bachelor, of middle stature, but very thin, being of a weakly constitution, and quite superannuated three or four years before his death. He died on the 18th of July, 1742, in the 91st year of his age. He engaged or employed four or five different rooms or apartments in his house for different purposes, into which none of the family could enter at any time without his permission. He was rarely visited at any time, except by two gentlemen of Bradford, one a mathematician, and the other an ingenious apothecary. They were admitted by the signal of rubbing a stone against a certain part of the outside of the house. He attended the Unitarian Chapel at Bradford, of which he was a member, and every Sunday he took care to be provided with plenty of halfpence, which he very charitably suffered to be taken singly out of his hand, held behind him during his walk to the chapel, by the poor people who followed. He never looked back or asked a single question. Mr. Sharp was very irregular at his meals, and remarkably sparing in his manner. A little square hole, something like a window, made a communication between the room where he was generally employed in calculations and another chamber or room in the house where a servant could enter, and before the hole he contrived a slide. The servant always placed his victuals, without speaking or making the least noise, and when he had a little leisure time he visited his cupboard to see what it afforded to satisfy his hunger and thirst. But it often happened that the breakfast, dinner, and supper remained untouched by him, and when the servant had gone to remove what was left the philosopher was found to have been so deeply engaged in his calculations that he had quite forgotten all about his meals.

Bradford. JOHN CLARK.

A BRADFORD WORTHY.

ARCHBISHOP SHARP was a native of Bradford, and was born on Shrove Tuesday, 1644. He was sent to school in his native town, and his father taught him shorthand for the particular purpose of taking down every Sunday the sermons he heard in church, and reading them to the family in the evening. In 1660, when fifteen years of age, Sharp was sent to Christ's College, Cambridge, for a University education. Whilst at college he was not idle, for, in addition to classics and divinity, he seemed to have been fond of chemistry and botany. He confessed that he knew but little of mathematics, but he was a devoted admirer of a work which no feeble intellect could grasp—the " Principia " of Sir Isaac Newton. In 1667 he left college and came home to Bradford, to take the chance of securing some stray piece of preferment in his native county. Soon after he was appointed domestic chaplain and tutor in the family of Sir Heneage Finch, who became his patron and lifelong friend. Whilst teaching he continued his own studies, in which his patron assisted him, Under such a roof Sharp's promotion was rapid. He was appointed to a stall at Norwich, and to the rectory of St. Giles's-in-the Fields, in London. It was as rector that he first won fame. As a preacher he was especially renowned. He prospered in the world, and in 1691, when he was Dean of Canterbury, he succeeded Thomas Lamplugh to the see of York, The English Church had then two Yorkshiremen at its head—Tillotson and Sharp. Both sprang from West Riding families, and both were deeply attached to their native county. The Yorkshire School, or, as it was then called, the Yorkshire Society, was established in London by them. At York he was a diligent pastor. He laid down a strict rule that no one but a Yorkshireman of approved character should have a Yorkshire benefice that he could give. He took care that the incumbent of the leading church in each Yorkshire town should hold a stall in the neighbouring cathedral. In looking after his diocese and the clergy, no one could be more gentle and at the same time more firm. He knew everything about his clergy, and they could talk to him as to a father. He was at all times ready with kindly advice, and taught by example as well as by precept. In politics he was a moderate Tory, but he shrank from political warfare on every occasion. Sharp's works are principally sermons, and at one time he was remarkably prolific. One of his favourite pursuits was collecting coins, of which he had a large and valuable store ; and he was a great friend of Ralph Thoresby, of Leeds. He died at Bath, whither he had gone in the vain hope of restoring his shattered health, on the 2nd February, 1713, and was buried on the 16th in his own Minster at York.

York.   JAS. WILLIAMSON.

JOSEPH GILLOTT

OF the many thousands of Yorkshire men and women who are daily in the habit of wielding that small but powerful instrument, the steel pen, probably few are aware that the most successful manufacturer of this useful and necessary article was a Yorkshireman. It is difficult to say what we should have done had not the invention of steel pens come just when it did. When Rowland Hill gave us the inestimable boon of penny postage, an impetus was given to writing and correspondence which could not have been sustained if all the geese in the world had been called upon to sacrifice their quills to meet the emergency. One writer has said that if Byron had lived a little later on, his celebrated couplet would not have apostrophised the " gray goose quill," but would probably have run something like this :—

> My Gillott pen ! thou noblest work of skill,
> Slave of my thoughts, obedient to my will.

Joseph Gillott was born at Sheffield, in October, 1799, of poor parents, who, notwithstanding their straitened circumstances, contrived to give their boy a good plain education, and also instilled into his mind the duty of self-reliance. They taught him, too, to train and cultivate the fine faculty of observation with which he had come into the world. When very young, we are told he, by forging and grinding the blades of pen-knives, contributed greatly to the income of the parental household, and also that his quick perception and his acute nervous organisation enabled him to produce much finer work than others of far greater experience in the same trade, whose obtuseness and indifference had kept them, as it daily keeps thousands, in a state of comparative drudgery all their lives.

When he was twenty-one years of age, the cutlery trade in Sheffield being much depressed, young Gillott went to Birmingham and commenced the manufacture of steel buckles and other articles of polished steel for personal adornment. He had no capital, but great skill. He was an excellent workman, and possessing as he did a great amount of " taste," he soon obtained abundance of orders, and became prosperous. At this time the steel pen trade—no insignificant branch of the steel manufacture at the present day—was in a tentative condition. Josiah Mason and Perry of the *Morning Chronicle* newspaper, were experimenting, and two brothers, named respectively John and William Mitchell, were actually making, by a tedious method, a fairly good article. They were assisted in their work by a sister. By some fortunate accident Gillott and Miss Mitchell met, and the "old, old story" being in their case soon told, they entered into an engagement to marry. She told her intended husband of her occupation, and Gillott at once conceived the idea that the *press*, the useful implement of the button trade, might, with some new tools to suit, produce pens in large numbers very rapidly. With his own hands, in the "upper room" of his house, he secretly worked until he had mastered the difficulty, and could, unassisted, produce as many pens as twenty pairs of hands under the old system could turn out. There was an enormous demand for his goods, and as he wanted help and secrecy was a *sine qua non*, the young couple married; and in after life Mr. Gillott used to tell how, on the wedding morning, before going to church, he made with his own hands a gross of pens, and sold them at one shilling each, realising thereby the sum of seven pounds four shillings.

Living in a small house in Bread Street, Gillott and his wife worked in the garret, no one else assisting. The manufacture of steel pens was then only in a crude state, for they were "blued" and varnished in a common fryingpan over a kitchen fire. Such, however, was the demand, and the goods were produced in such quantities, that the young couple made money faster than they knew what to do with it. They were afraid to invest it, as it might tell of large profits, so Mr. Gillott opened several banking accounts, being afraid that if he paid all his profits into one bank it might excite cupidity and so bring about competition. In the course of a few years he built large factories, and then commenced to advertise extensively, a practice which he continued during the remainder of his life. More than forty years ago I remember to have seen his short but pithy advertisements in the cheap magazines then being issued by Charles Knight and others. The number of pens produced by Gillott in 1836 was 36,000,000. By means of labour-saving machinery which Gillott introduced, the price of the pens fell from one shilling each to less than that sum per gross, and the steel pen came into universal use. At the time of Mr. Gillott's death the number of pens produced weekly at his works was something enormous, and can scarcely be set down in figures. The average weight of the weekly make exceeded five tons, and would give a result in numbers of something like sixty thousand gross, or nine million separate pens sent out from this manufactory every week.

As I am not anxious in this sketch to write simply of the history of the trade in steel pens, but rather to speak of Mr. Gillott himself, and draw some lessons from his life, I would say that one of his chief characteristics was his love of excellence in everything with which he had to do. He went in for quality in his pens rather than lowness of price, and in all the affairs of life it was a joke of his that " the best of everything was good enough for him." He earnestly carried out in life the desire to do and possess the " best " that could be attained. His love of beautiful flowers and plants was very marked, and he had a fancy for collecting precious stones, simply as rarities. He also accumulated a very large and fine collection of violins and stringed musical instruments, which, when sold by auction after his death, realised upwards of £4,000. Known throughout the world as a successful manufacturer, he was almost equally renowned as a most munificent and discriminating patron of art. He could instinctively recognise the *true* in the work of young artists, and always encouraged the budding talent. Müller, a gifted genius, came in for a share of his warm support, but he scarcely repaid Gillott in a generous way. By reason of Gillott's patronage, others sought the young artist and bought at large prices the pictures which had been commissioned by his patron, and in other ways Müller managed to annoy his friend. But the punishment was swift, severe, and sure. Gillott immediately packed off to London every Müller picture he possessed, for sale by auction, and sold without the slightest reserve. This step so frightened the art-world that " Müllers " became a drug in the market, and the disappointed artist went in penitence to Gillott, who again took him by the hand, and befriended him until his untimely death in 1845, at the age of 33. At the sale of Mr. Gillott's pictures Müller's celebrated picture, " The Chess Players," realised the large sum of £3,950.

The story of Mr. Gillott's introduction to the great landscape painter, Turner, is worthy of record. It seems that the wealthy manufacturer, long before Ruskin had styled Turner " the modern

Claude," had detected the rare excellence of his works, and longed to possess some. He went to the dingy house in Queen Anne Street, and the great painter himself opened the door. In reply to Gillott's questions, he said he had "nothing to sell that *he* could afford to buy." Gillott, by a good deal of manœuvring, obtained admission, and tried at first to bargain for a single picture. Turner looked disdainfully at his visitor, and refused to quote a price. Still Gillott persevered, and at length startled the artist by asking, "What'll you take for the lot in this room?" Turner, half-jokingly, named a very large sum—many thousands—thinking to frighten him off, but Gillott opened his pocket book, and, to Turner's utter amazement, paid down the money in crisp Bank of England notes. This was the beginning of a lasting friendship. Gillott's collection of Turner's works was the largest and finest in private hands in England, and, when they were sold, realised more than five times the money he had paid for them.

Mr. Gillott was not what is known as a public man, and took no active part in politics. He had a sensible dislike to public companies, and never held a share in one. He was very hospitable, but disliked formal parties and every kind of ostentation. In private life he was cheerful, easily pleased, and unaffected. Mr. Gillott departed this life on the afternoon of Friday, the 5th of January, 1873, closing in peace a long, honourable, and useful life.

Morley, near Leeds.   THE EDITOR.

CHARLES FORREST

DURING the month of October, 1871, the Yorkshire newspapers recorded the death of the gifted antiquary, Mr. Charles Forrest, a gentleman who did much for the local history and topography of Yorkshire. He was a native of the Forest of Knaresborough, and was brought up by his grandfather, at Whitwell Nook, about six miles from Harrogate. His early education was received at West House School, afterwards at Burnt Yates School, under the tuition of the late Mr. William Cockett. For a short time Mr. Forrest was a schoolmaster in the village of Birstwith. Afterwards he obtained an appointment under the late John Charlesworth, Esq , and removed to Lofthouse, near Wakefield, where he resided more than thirty years. Three generations of the family of Charlesworth were faithfully served by him. In early life his love for antiquities and local history was developed, and he attributed the taste for such studies to the perusal of "Hargrove's History of Knaresborough." He had a most extensive bibliographical knowledge, and owned one of the best collections of Yorkshire books that has been made, as a private library. Not only did he collect books, but made in them most carefully written notes, and in many instances illustrated them with photographs, sketches, and prints. Mr. Forrest made a number of books with newspaper cuttings, which were carefully indexed and bound in the best style. Two or three of these books occur to our mind: "Yorkshire Longevity," "Yorkshire Customs," and another, the "History of Castleford." Had he been spared, we believe he would have written a history of Castleford. Ever ready to place his books at the disposal of his friends and to give information, his assistance was often sought. The late W. S. Banks, in his "Walks in Yorkshire;" William Grainge, in his "Poets and Poetry of Yorkshire," and other works; Abraham Holroyd, in his "Bradford Collectanea," as well as many others, express their obligations for his kindly help. He frequently contributed antiquarian and biographical sketches to the various journals. In conjunction with his friend, William Grainge, he published "Rambles on Rumbolds Moor," which extended to three parts : the first appeared in 1867, the second in 1868, and the last in 1869, giving an account of the early British antiquities of that district. The last was more especially devoted to the sculptured rocks then recently discovered near the village of Ilkley, and to which it was the means of drawing the attention of the antiquarian world. To the end of life Mr. Forrest took a lively interest in antiquarian pursuits. A sketch of the "Life of Hopkinson, the Lofthouse Antiquary and Genealogist of the 17th Century," was compiled by him. He wrote "History and Antiquities of Knottingley," a valuable local work, which was published after the death of the author. Besides his knowledge of bibliography and archæology, Mr. Forrest was also skilled in architecture and natural history. Of botany, the ferns formed his particular study, of which he had a choice selection, both English and foreign. Mr. Grainge- tells us Mr. Forrest was in the habit of keeping a diary, in which all transactions of a literary or scientific kind were carefully recorded. He also preserved the correspondence of his literary friends, which at one time was somewhat extensive. His bodily strength for some years was not robust, yet he could endure a considerable amount of labour, as was shown in many a long ramble over rough roads, and sometimes over no roads at all, among rocks and mountains, in pursuit of his favourite studies. He was an early riser, and remarkably temperate in his habits ; and if he was extravagant in anything it was in books. In the beginning of June, 1871, he was struck down by illness, and for some weeks suffered very severely, being confined to his room; afterwards he rallied, and his friends began to hope that he would be spared to them a little longer. He tried the air of Ilkley— the fresh breezes of which had often renovated his failing strength— but in vain. He returned home in August, no better, but weaker, than he went. At that time it was painfully apparent to his friends that the hand of death was upon him. He, however, lingered, sometimes suffering severely. but gradually sinking, until the morning of October 24th, when he died, and on the 28th was buried at Rothwell.

Hull.   W. ANDREWS, F.R.H.S.

HENRY STOOKS SMITH

O mundi tautorum caussa laborum,
Quid superos et fata tems ? Sunt cætera cursu
Acta meo.

ON the 19th February, 1881, there died at Headingley, in the 73rd year of his age, one of the remarkable men of Leeds, Henry Stooks Smith.   It is not given to all men to be original and eccentric, to be painstaking and laborious, to be diligent, untiring and yet enthusiastic in the pursuit of his favourite studies ; and yet it was his lot to be all these.   The son of a Leeds wool merchant, the lad was sent at an early age into Germany, to be educated for his father's business. But from his very boyhood trade was to him an uncongenial thing ; he had been endowed with the spirit of a soldier, and for his whole life soldier-craft was his absorbing passion.   Mixing in his boyhood, both at home and abroad, with the heroes of the great war, whose society he carefully sought and cultivated, and largely enjoyed, he became the repository of the unwritten stories of hundreds of gallant acts, and the friend of those more fortunate ones, whose fame Napier, his correspondent, has chronicled in immortal history.   For some time in his young manhood Mr. Smith was engaged in trade, but he did not long continue it.   In 1845-6 he commenced sharebroking in partnership with Mr. Perfect, but that he soon discontinued, and, falling back upon a moderate competency, which he materially increased with great facility amongst his numerous influential friends, by an agency of the "Royal" Fire and Life Insurance Company, he thenceforth gave himself up to the prosecution of his favourite studies.

Born in the ranks of unmitigated Toryism, cherished by the recollections of their transient splendour, and soured by his personal conflicts in their defeats, politics and Toryism were to him the very breath of life.   Contempt that could not be spoken possessed him for those of ideas opposite to his own.   In his boyhood he had friends, intimate and confidential, of whom two became illustrious members of Parliament for his native borough, and one of them venerated, as good men are venerated, yet the point of divergence in their boyish opinions was never forgotten, and the position they came to hold in the progress of affairs was to him the crowning scandal of a false judgment.   From the Reform Bill of 1832 to the moment of his death he was a county voter, and, more, a determined and vigorous supporter of his political creed.   As a Tory he, of course, was a Churchman, of the free, but robust type, which prevailed a century ago, with the utmost abhorrence of Puritanical manners and dissent of every kind.   His most withering scorn was wont to culminate in the denunciation of people whom he considered strait-laced, as " Radicals, Teetotallers, and misery-mongers." But, though an ardent politician and an active worker at elections, he always steadily declined to accept any office.

It was not, however, as a politician that he deserves to be remembered, but as an author and book collector, and, though he was both these, it was impossible to call him literary. His efforts in authorship, which resulted in some ten or a dozen volumes, were, except to specialists, as he himself was, not of an interesting kind. His greatest work, " The Parliaments of England," 3 vols. 8vo, giving the names of members and candidates of all the elections in England and Wales from 1716 to the date of publication, in 1848 or 9, was well reviewed and spoken of as a "useful work to the publicist, and to all persons interested in Parliamentary matters," all of which it undoubtedly is, yet the book fell flat from the press. "It is not easy to conceive the vast expenses, pains, and troubles attending searches of this nature," and in the production of the book none of these were spared. But, if the labour was enormous, the subject was uninvitiug, and capable only of producing a dry catalogue of names and a list of figures; of the greatest utility indeed to those who knew how to use it, but affording no more reading than a table of logarithms or a ready-reckoner. Apart from its uninviting subject, the great merit of the book is in its completeness and unfailing accuracy. From it Mr. Smith turned to the compilation of the lists of officers of every regiment in the Army from 1800 to date of publication, of which he published seven volumes. These, especially the earlier ones, like his other work, " The Parliaments of England," were merely a catalogue of names and dates, those of the commissions, promotions, retirements, and places of death. As works of reference they are invaluable, and in future years will help many a pedigree manufacturer to dates and facts that he would not elsewhere have been able to obtain, yet of biographical matter which alone could have rendered them interesting, they contain the sparsest amount. It was with the utmost difficulty that the writer prevailed upon Mr. Smith to admit into his later volumes even the scant notices contained in Hart's " Army List"; having done so he had to confess that the sale of these books reached the price of publication, which was far from the case in the earlier volumes. In 1854 he commenced the publication of " The Military Obituary," the year 1853 starting the series. This publication, which he hoped to carry on year by year, gave the services of all present and past officers whose deaths were recorded   It was continued for six years, the year 1857 being the last published, when it died as an expensive and unappreciated effort. It was to him, having lost many hundreds of pounds in the production of his books, a grim satisfaction to know that they were like port wine, they would improve by keeping and become priceless with age, as he used to console himself by stating.

As a book collector Mr. Smith collected a library of about 10,000 volumes, chiefly military and topographical. At one time these collections were famous, but a few years before his death he was induced to part with the best of them by the offer of high prices, and so at the sale of his effects the cream of his library was gone.

But it was not either as author or collector that he will only be remembered. He has a claim upon us as the founder of the Leeds Rifles. It was he, in connection with the late A. Horsfall, solicitor, who took the first steps, but the initiation of the thing was undoubtedly due to Mr. Smith, who had no sooner developed the idea than he constituted himself recruiting sergeant (or rather private, for during his long service in the corps he never would advance beyond that grade), and worked most assiduously until he had secured the nucleus of the splendid regiment which now remains as a monument to his influence and patriotism.

Mr. Smith never married; it was said that he was the victim of unrequited love in his younger days; he had all, and more than all, an old bachelor's horror of the blandishments of the gentle sex, whose society he would not encourage or even tolerate. Practically living alone, for he had but a housekeeper near him, and very few friends whose society he cultivated, it may be said that he ended his life among his books, in the seclusion of a hermit and the moroseness of age, having out-lived nearly the whole of his contemporaries, and shunning with a morbid pride, the excrescence of his Toryism, those around him who had so greatly risen from the station he had known their fathers in.

Leeds.   W. WHEATER.